GOOD SHOOTING

GOOD SHOOTING

J. E. M. Ruffer

Illustrated by John Catchpole

DAVID & CHARLES
Newton Abbot   London   North Pomfret (Vt)

British Library Cataloguing in Publication Data

Ruffer, John Edward Maurice
  Good shooting.
  1. Shooting
  I. Title ˙
  799.2'13   GV1153

  ISBN 0-7153-7917-8

Parts of this book appeared previously under the title *The Art of Good Shooting*, first published in 1972 and revised in 1976

Library of Congress Catalog Card Number: 79–56044

© J. E. M. Ruffer 1980

Typeset by
Northern Phototypesetting Company Bolton
and printed in Great Britain
by Biddles Limited Guildford Surrey
for David & Charles (Publishers) Limited
Brunel House Newton Abbot Devon

Published in the United States of America
by David & Charles Inc
North Pomfret Vermont 05053 USA

Contents

Acknowledgements

Some of the material in this book has already appeared in *The Shooting Times & Country Magazine*. I am most grateful to the Editor, Tony Jackson, for his kind permission to reproduce it. My thanks are due also to the British Field Sports Society for their agreement for part of their pamphlet *This is Grouse Shooting* to be reproduced here.

John Catchpole is the artist of the line drawings: it is a pity that his shooting is only nearly as good as his artistic ability. Roy Shaw took most of the photographs: he is an expert fisherman as well. Finally, I must thank Wendy McCormick for her typing. Her enthusiasm and speed has made the whole thing possible – and she could often read my handwriting first time!

Photographs are reproduced by permission of the following:
John Catchpole: pp 29, 30, 44–5, 50, 161, 176
James and John Marchington: p 21 (top and bottom left)
Roy Shaw: pp 20, 21 (bottom right), 34, 37, 40, 41, 48, 53, 55, 67, 70, 80, 81, 92, 136, 150, 151, 153, 154, 160, 163, 165, 169, 172

Introduction

Books on sport are usually written by tournament winners, or those most successful in competitions. They are, of course, acknowledged experts. But it is one thing to be good at a sport. It is quite another to be able to tell other people how to do it.

There are, on the other hand, people who are really keen on a sport, often quite good at it. They may also have one prime asset so far as someone else is concerned: they enjoy teaching. I belong to this category.

And if you enjoy teaching, you cannot fail to become quite an expert at it. This is perhaps because the whole business of teaching makes you tackle the problem from a different angle. The average shot goes to a coach to find out what he is doing wrong. I – if I can teach at all – have to analyse everything so that it is done correctly. In short, I work for what is right.

We all know the days when you can hit anything that comes. Most of us do not worry about days like this; but this is just when I – as an instructor – do think and analyse what I have been doing to make things go right. And so I now know what has to be done to shoot correctly. In short, I can make the good days repeat. And, after all, a good shot is a man who shoots well when he is shooting badly.

There is one step further for any instructor, and that is to convey his knowledge to his pupil. This is very difficult, since it requires constant repetition and practice before any result is achieved. It is comparatively easy with young people; it is sometimes almost impossible with older poeple. Why is this? It is basically because the older person thinks he is doing something that he has been told – is positively certain of it – when in fact he is not. In short *merely* to read this book is a waste of time. *You must practise what is preached.* This can usually be done in your bedroom, by yourself, with the help of a looking-glass.

Furthermore, you should not despise the clay pigeon and the shooting school. I myself do as much shooting as I can. I also frequently go to a shooting school. Occasionally when out shooting, I meet the really first-class shot – of whom there are remarkably few! When I later mention his name in conversation to my shooting instructor, that good shot is *invariably* well known at the shooting schools. If *he* thinks it worth it, how much more profitable must it be for us lesser mortals? No one man is a better shot than another! It is simply that the good shot makes it easier for himself, and this is an art that can be taught, and learnt quite easily.

This will not be believed. Someone will quickly tell of exceptions. Take, for example, they will say, the few men and boys who have very bad co-ordination. They cannot shoot well, and never will. This does not disprove what I say. I repeat, to be a good shot you have only to make it easier for yourself. Some people find the rules which make it easier for themselves hard to learn; they merely take longer to become good shots.

Of course, the people who learn quickest are the young. They learn quickly and soon become good shots and, what is more, they never forget. I once coached a boy of about seventeen who had never shot before. I told him what to do, and he did it exactly. He never missed! He never looked as if he would miss. (He did not come back. He was not very keen on shooting – a pity!)

Everything in this book is therefore written with the idea of making the whole thing easier for you. You may not believe that it is *only* making it easier for yourself that makes you a good shot. Let me give you an example of what I mean. I was out one day at Grantham where there was one young man shooting who played cricket for England. He did not hit much. The next-door 'gun', a port-sodden old boy of sixty, scarcely missed anything all day. The old man, although pathetically unfit, having slow reactions, and being half blind, knew enough about making it easier for himself to shoot well. The young man did not know and, in spite of his complete physical fitness and mental co-ordination, shot badly. Think how well the young man could have shot if he had known the tricks of the trade.

Some of us know the day when we cannot miss. Equally we all know the day when we even hope the birds will not come our way. The average shot is somewhere in between, and knows both ecstasy and despair.

Remember that definition of a good shot as the man who shoots well when he is shooting badly. I am going to teach you never to shoot badly. You will then quickly get a reputation – for what that is worth – of being a good shot. It is interesting that people always notice the man who is shooting well, and often do not spot the man 'off his day'. Not 'interesting', perhaps, so much as merciful.

1 Handling Your Gun

How the gun works

A shotgun is like any other hand weapon: it is designed to harness the potential energy contained in the modern cartridge. The gun is useless without the cartridge, and of course the cartridge is not much good without the gun.

The cartridge has a detonator which explodes very rapidly indeed when it is struck a sharp blow. The detonator in turn ignites the propelling powder, which pushes the shot load comparatively slowly out of the barrel. The shot consists of lead pellets, the number varying with their size and the size of the gun but probably averaging about 300. The shotgun pellets cannot fall out before firing because the end of the cartridge is crimped over; and they are not melted by the hot powder because there is a protecting wad.

So much for the cartridge. The average sporting shotgun usually has two barrels, placed side by side. These barrels fit into the 'action', which in turn is attached to the 'stock'. The whole is held firmly together by the 'fore-end', which snaps on to the barrels and the action.

The object of the barrels, which are smooth inside, is to contain the force of the explosion when the cartridge is fired, and then direct the shot in one direction only – up the barrels, which hopefully are directed accurately towards the target. Although the barrels are fixed to the action and stock, they are hinged downwards and the fore-end allows the gun to be opened just wide enough for the cartridge to be inserted. When the gun is then closed, the hammers in the action are cocked, and will fly forward to detonate the cartridge when the triggers – one for each barrel, and also attached to the action – are pulled. When the gun is opened after firing, the hammers are again cocked, and

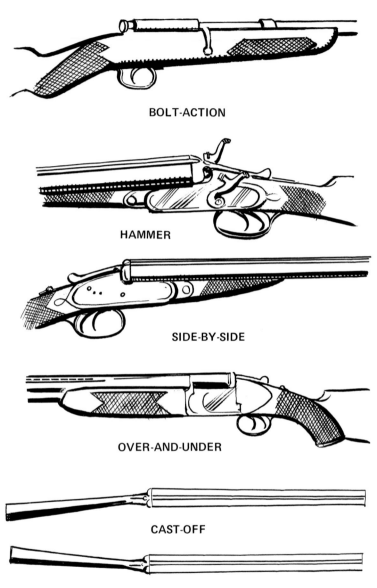

BOLT-ACTION

HAMMER

SIDE-BY-SIDE

OVER-AND-UNDER

CAST-OFF

CAST-ON

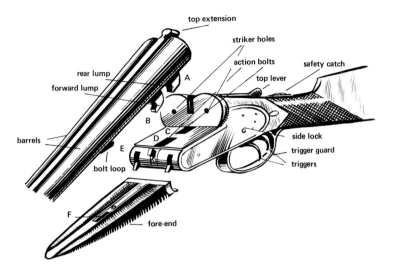

top extension

striker holes

action bolts

safety catch

rear lump

forward lump

top lever

A

barrels

B

C

side lock

trigger guard

triggers

D

E

bolt loop

F

fore-end

When gun is fitted together, A goes into C, B into D, and E into F on fore-end

the fired cartridge may be ejected. One common term which perhaps requires some explanation is 'hammerless': this simply means that the hammers are invisible inside the action.

It is of course possible to include all sorts of personal requirements such as single triggers, engraving and so on. Some guns are made with the barrels 'over and under' instead of side by side; and all barrels may be constricted slightly at the muzzle to prevent the shot charge spreading unduly at longer ranges.

The most usual size of sporting gun is the 12-bore. The bore is measured by the number of lead balls, made to fit the barrel exactly, which make up 1lb avoirdupois: thus if there are twelve lead balls to the pound, the size of a single ball gives the size of a 12-bore gun. Twenty lead balls to the pound give the size of a 20-bore gun – obviously smaller. The actual diameter of the bore of a 12-guage gun is about .729in, and of a 20-bore about .615in. The only gun that does not comply with the old-fashioned system of measurement is the 'four-ten', which is actually named for the diameter of its bore – .410in.

All guns have to stand the force of the explosion with something to spare: to achieve this, they are 'proofed', and if 'in proof' will be absolutely safe – unless the barrel is blocked – from any danger of bursting. Sporting guns are therefore expensive. They will be very expensive indeed if hand-made, as 'best' guns are; they are much cheaper if mass-produced.

There are variations in almost infinite number on this description: there are single-barrelled guns; automatics which will fire up to five rounds; hammer guns where the hammers have to be cocked, i.e. pulled back by hand; and even bolt-action guns which work like rifles. But the average sporting gun is a 12-bore side-by-side double-barrelled hammerless ejector gun.

Holding the gun

There are, of course, correct and incorrect ways of holding a gun. When I say holding, I mean before mounting the gun to your cheek and shoulder. I do not mean how to carry it, which I shall describe under 'safety'. I am going to assume that you shoot from the right shoulder. If you shoot from the left, then for 'left hand' read 'right hand' throughout.

The left hand holds the gun at the fore-end. The actual position of the hand on the fore-end, or even beyond on the barrels, is important and we will discuss this in a moment.

Try to keep the thumb and fingers off the top of the barrels. Although I will repeatedly say that you do not look at the gun barrels when you are pointing and mounting (and firing) at the birds, a 'heavy' grip with fingers and thumb on top of the barrels tends to distort one's instinctive pointing sense, so keep them out of the way.

The right hand grasps the small of the butt, with the forefinger – trigger finger – on the trigger guard. The right hand should tend to be under the gun; if it is not, it will force the right elbow up as the gun comes into the cheek and shoulder. This in turn will tend to make it difficult to push the gun forward towards the bird. You will tend to lift the gun, instead of pushing it towards the bird.

Let us make it easy for ourselves, and keep the right hand

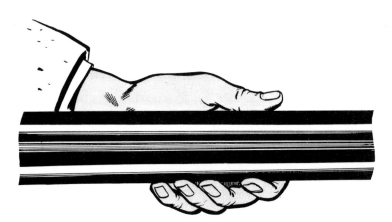

Try to keep the thumb off the top of the barrels

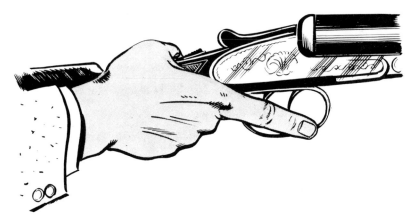

The right hand grasps the small of the butt, with the forefinger on the trigger guard. The hand should tend to be under the gun. The thumb must be round the stock, not on top

under rather than on top of the gun. The thumb must be round the stock – not on top. There is a tendency, as you move the safety catch from 'safe' prior to firing, for the thumb to remain there. If this is done, there are three disadvantageous effects:

(a) You lose some of the right hand's control.
(b) Under certain conditions – slack grip, too short a stock – the recoil will cause the end of the top lever to be forced back

The 'ready' position: gun roughly horizontal, pointing to where you expect the bird; stock tucked and gripped under the fore-arm

on to the end of your right thumb, and may even split it or bruise it badly.

(c) If your thumb is left on the safety catch, the recoil of the first shot may well cause you unknowingly to re-apply the safety catch, and you will then be unable to fire the second barrel. (As this happens without your being aware of it, you may well be convinced that the gun is defective – and it can be quite expensive to have a perfectly good safety catch 'repaired'.)

Do not have the right hand too far forward, that is, with the rear of the trigger guard pressing hard up against the second finger. This is sometimes done in order that the front trigger may be pulled with the *joint* of the first finger. Make sure that you pull the trigger with the ball of the first finger; to achieve this, you will have to pull your right hand back a shade. Then all bruising of the second finger from the back of the trigger guard will disappear.

Now, where should you place your left hand on the fore-end? Mount the gun by pointing and pushing the gun towards the target. The butt should just clear your clothing as it comes up into your shoulder and cheek. If it seems to catch, bring the left hand back a bit. If the butt obviously clears the clothing by a good gap, push your left hand a little further up the barrels.

Provided that the length of the stock is about right, you can thus compensate for wearing heavy shooting clothes or not, simply by altering the position of your left hand on the barrels. More important, this is the best way of compensating for shooting with the same gun with longer arms, which occurs when you are growing!

The length of the stock should allow you to hold the gun towards the front end of the fore-end. If the stock is much too long, you will be forced to hold the gun with the left hand too far back and at once you can feel that the gun is then more difficult to control.

It is also important to adopt a good position for the gun as soon as you realise that game is about to get up, or is approaching. I

17

realise that it is virtually impossible to appreciate exactly when game is 'about to get up'. This is only one reason why rough shooting and walking up is more difficult than many would have us believe. All the same, if you do get warning – and you usually do, at least in the case of driven game – then it will pay you to adopt a position that will help you even before you are able to see the bird.

The object of good mounting is to get the gun pointing and moving towards the bird as soon as possible. You must therefore adopt a preliminary position to ensure that the barrels have a short distance to go to the bird – the shorter the better.

Take up a position with the gun roughly horizontal, with the stock tucked and gripped under the right fore-arm. In the case of a high bird approaching, adopt the same position with the barrels cocked up a bit. The barrels now have only a short distance to go to any bird approaching, and you can more easily fulfil the criterion of mounting with the bird (see next section, 'Gun Mounting').

Many of us start off with the barrels pointing downwards. Consider how far the barrels have to move before they are pointing at the bird. This makes it more difficult to point and push forward at the bird. Make it easier for yourself by starting with the gun somewhere near where the bird is going to be.

Do not stand with the gun at the 'high port' position, especially when expecting a lowish bird. The barrels then have to come *down* towards the bird, whereas the bird, if it is up in the air at all, appears to require the barrels to be moving *up* to keep with it. This 'high port' position, therefore, does not make it easier for yourself. It is often adopted by the pheasant shot when shooting grouse for the first time. When you see him with his gun like this on a grouse moor, it is a fairly safe bet that he is about to make a hash of his first day's grouse shooting.

Adopt the position I have suggested if you can. You can go straight to the bird then, with the minimum of effort. You are making it easy for yourself. I appreciate that there are many occasions when this position just is not possible. When trying to

18

keep hidden, for instance, and often when walking up. In these cases, you must accept this disadvantage. But do not accept such a disadvantage when you do not have to.

Gun mounting

I believe that all men and women have innate abilities which can make it possible for them to do things much better – or even to do them at all in the first place – if only they will let them. There is of course one other requirement for the fruition of these talents: we must fervently wish to do that which we may be capable of doing. A potentially great pianist, for example, must *want* to play the piano.

The trouble with intelligent man is that his reasoning so very often prevents him from using the powers that he actually possesses in abundance. How long, for example, did it take man to realise he could ride a bicycle? Thousands of years! And solely because his reasoning told him that it was not possible to stay upright on two wheels.

We are of course leading up to shooting. What is true of riding a bike is true basically of shooting: shooting can be done very well, very easily. We *have* to ride a bicycle well, or we will fall off and hurt ourselves and we are frightened of doing this. But we do not *have* to shoot very well, although many of us want to. This is really why there are not a great many more good shots about, in spite of the fact that virtually all of us have the innate ability to achieve a really extraordinary standard of marksmanship.

How then do we set about releasing this ability, which I repeat we all possess? The obvious way of learning is not necessarily the easiest way. If you come to think of it, the 'obvious' way to learn to ride a bike would be to sit on a stationary machine and try to stay upright by 'balancing' it: to try and start learning with the thing moving would be suicidal, surely! It is the same with shooting. Common sense, logic, call it what you will, insists that you should have to aim when you are shooting, and virtually everyone teaches this. Only two people in the world, that I know

19

of, have realised that this is basically difficult, and can only
achieve limited success.

The easy way to shoot well
I say that there must be an easy way, otherwise the really good
shots, of which there are certainly some, simply could not shoot
as well as they do.

Put the gun to the bird and pull the trigger. Try to mount with
the bird: it will work.

That is the answer! Having read that, you will probably put
this book down with a look of blank incomprehension. What
about lead, the long crossing shot, the curving grouse – and on
and on, *ad infinitum*? But can you not see that when you talk like
this, you are merely being the logical, sensible man telling us all,
yourself included, that it is obviously impossible to ride a bicycle!
It is impossible if you try to ride one stationary; shooting is
difficult if you try to do it by aiming.

20

Point at it . . .

mount with it . . .

and this will happen!

It has been said that good gun mounting is half the battle to good shooting. It is more; it is very nearly all the battle. Learn good and correct gun mounting, and you are a very long way down the road to the goal of making it easy for yourself.

Now, how to do it correctly. My explanation may sound complicated, but the execution itself is easy.

One factor is paramount: *your gun must be with the bird all the time you mount.* To achieve this, your gun mounting must be unhurried. The man who snatches his gun to his shoulder has as much chance of keeping the gun with the bird as he mounts as of swimming the Channel with roller skates.

To achieve this 'gun with the bird' effect, you must point your gun deliberately at the bird as you mount. Just as you instinctively straighten your arm when you point with your finger, so I want you to feel as if you were straightening your arms towards the target as you mount. It feels as if you were pushing your gun forward towards the bird – as indeed you are. You must do this instinctively, *without* looking at your barrels.

You may ask how anyone can point his gun at the target before it gets to his shoulder, without looking at the barrels. Well, point with your finger at any object in your room; instinctively you point straight at the object, straightening your arm as you do so, without looking at your finger. And if you subsequently sight along your finger, you will find you are dead on.

The same applies if you visualise the gun barrels as your finger. Point them at the bird, by pushing the gun forward, making a strong effort to point at the bird all the time you are mounting. This is really the difficult part. It is not difficult to *do*; the trouble is that you *think* you are pointing all the time you are mounting, but often you are not!

To achieve this, both hands must mount the gun together; one hand must not move faster than the other. If it does, the gun will see-saw and obviously will not be with the bird. There is a very strong tendency for this to happen, since the impulse is for the right hand to snatch the butt up into the shoulder. Down go the

Your gun must be with the bird all the time you mount

Point your gun deliberately at the bird as you mount

Your gun must be on the target all the time you mount

barrels, and your weapon is see-sawing only vaguely towards the target. Mount the gun 'all of a piece'.

Do all this without haste. The slower your mounting, before the gun gets into your shoulder, the easier it is to mount with the bird. You will not jerk the barrels off the bird, and you can concentrate on mounting smoothly and unhurriedly with the bird. But, you may say, the bird does not give you time for all this. (In fact it nearly always does.) The point I am making — rather laboriously perhaps — is that you must learn to do it properly, and it is easier if you start slowly. So choose your starling, say, some way off, coming slowly towards you; this will give you time to practise.

Notice that I have told you to mount the gun 'with the bird'. I mean this literally — certainly with no lead (forward allowance) yet. As the gun comes into the shoulder, it is, if you are still with the bird, easy to move the gun fractionally ahead of the bird and pull the trigger. This is really easy, as the extra movement is minute at the gun end — your end.

When you do this, you quite unconsciously carry out all the maxims that the gun experts say should be followed when shooting:

(a) You have not checked (you *cannot* if you keep with the bird).
(b) You are achieving an accelerating swing.
(c) You are pulling the trigger when the gun comes into the shoulder, and not dwelling on aim with the gun in your shoulder.

All this sounds appallingly complicated when you consider the limited time during which the bird is in shot, or approaching the shot. It is not. All you are doing, really, is to slow down your mounting, and speed up your trigger pull. Why do this? It has the most colossal advantage — and this is what we are here for!

If you mount the gun, and *then* aim with the gun already in your cheek and shoulder, you will never shoot well, quickly, or in good style. You are making it harder for yourself – something to be avoided at all costs. The reason is that if you mount any old how, you then have to *aim* with the gun in your shoulder. You are using it like a rifle: this is poking.

Style is very difficult to define, but it happens that good style looks right and bad style wrong. Aiming with the gun in your shoulder looks wrong and is, indeed, bad style. Using such a style makes it difficult for yourself, for as your brain says 'fire' you check – a fact of which you are quite unconscious. You are thus employing a decelerating swing of your gun, instead of an accelerating movement. So remember, push and point the gun at the bird, in the same way as you point with your finger, rather than lifting the gun to the target. If you lift the gun to a low bird, the momentum of two arms and the gun moving upwards tends to take the gun over a low-flying bird and you will have to correct, or miss over the top. In any case, you will be breaking the rule of keeping the gun pointing at the bird while you mount. In addition, lifting will almost inevitably cause the barrels to dip down as you mount the butt to your cheek. So do not lift the gun to the bird but *point* it by pushing it at the bird.

To sum up then, the actual mounting of the gun with the bird is vital. This is when you are 'aiming'. To get the maximum value, do not hurry it. You seldom have to, whatever you may feel. Then pull the trigger as the gun gets to your shoulder and cheek.

You may take a bit longer over the first stage, but this is time well spent, and you will more than save it on the second stage.

How to point
When I am coaching someone who is shooting beautifully at clays, I sometimes ask him how he thinks he is doing it. The usual reply I get is, 'I simply point the gun with my left hand (or both hands) as you have told me as I mount it, and then pull the trigger as it comes into my shoulder. What I can't understand is that the gun seems to be pointing only roughly at the bird.' Not to worry! Point the gun to the bird with the left hand – quickly or

slowly as required, but looking at the bird – and pull the trigger as it comes fully up. Not very difficult – almost as easy as riding a bicycle in fact!

It is on this basis that I try and make shooting easy for all those I teach – and of course for all those who read this book. I repeat that shooting is fundamentally easy because the average man has, in his brain, nerves and muscles, a fine machine designed to cope with just the sort of problems that shooting presents. Although no one would deny this, I have omitted one fundamental truth. The average man never uses the machine with which he is equipped. Shooting for the average man is thus not nearly as simple as it might be.

The snag is of course that the easiest way of shooting never has been taught, so far as I know. No one yet has really got down to the fundamentals of teaching people how to use the splendid co-ordination apparently designed specifically for shooting – which all of us possess.

Some have frequently come pretty close to the truth. I quote some examples, all of which are on the right lines; but the words, taken by themselves, are useless for teaching someone how to make the whole thing easy:

(a) 'Shoot instinctively.'
(b) 'Look at the bird.'
(c) 'Squirt at 'em.'
(d) 'I remember a friend who used to shoot very competently from the hip.'

The truth is there, but every quotation above contains only a part of the truth: no one has fitted it together and presented a gleaming certainty that the average man will believe.

The perfect machine that we possess is the ability to *point* our finger, or anything that we hold, at an object with considerable accuracy. It is easy. But when we are being taught to shoot, no one ever tells us to point; they all say 'swing'!

Point your finger quickly at anything instinctively; then look

28

Correct gun mounting

(*top left*) Gun 'ready' position

(*top right*) Bird sighted, gun being pushed and pointed at it

(*centre left*) Gun still 'pointing at target, not yet into cheek and shoulder

(*centre right*) Still pointing at target, eye on bird

(*left*) Gun mounted and fired. It has been with the target for the last three pictures

Incorrect gun mounting
(*top left*) 'Ready' position, gun already pointed towards probable position of game
(*top right*) 'Gun' sees target and instantly mounts his gun. Right hand pulls butt into cheek and barrels go down below target
(*centre left*) Aiming with gun already mounted, trying to get back on to target lost in previous picture
(*centre right*) Still having to aim
(*right*) At last on the target, but only momentarily

along it, and you are dead on. Next, take a walking stick, hold it in both hands and point it, without aiming or deliberately aligning it, at any object. Keep the stick still, and ask a friend to look along it, and once again it is plumb on target. It is just as easy if the object is moving: you can keep it on the object easily.

Now let us take the phrase 'squirt at 'em'. By themselves, would these words help you to shoot any better? They don't help me! But I surmise that someone once talked to a 'class' shot, and asked him how he did it – and received that reply. Dutifully he incorporated the phrase in a book, hoping perhaps that it would help someone. Let us clothe this phrase with an explanation, and then see if it will help.

Imagine you were shooting with a gun capable of projecting a very fast jet of water from its barrel. If you then mounted the gun, keeping the jet of water playing on the bird, all you would have to do on the gun getting into your shoulder and cheek would be to pull the trigger. Keeping the jet of water on the bird would be easy enough. And it is equally easy if the jet of water is imaginary! In other words, if you point the gun at the bird all the time you mount – which is truly easy – all you have to do is pull the trigger when the gun gets into shoulder and cheek.

If you comply with this advice, you are then making full use of the super machine which you possess. In fact it is *so* easy that most people cannot believe it. When the gun is finally mounted, they feel that some adjustment of the gun must be necessary, to make certain the gun is pointing as they think it should be. They hesitate, destroy all that their wonderful co-ordination has achieved, and miss.

This fault can be cured very easily. When a man who is mounting correctly is making this mistake, I ask him to press the trigger when I tell him to. As he mounts correctly with the gun pointing at the bird, I say 'Pull.' He fires and breaks the clay. He turns round and says, 'Bother me! It's not possible; I was nowhere near it.' Apart from two demonstrably incorrect facts in this short sentence, he is merely expressing his disbelief. And this disbelief would probably apply to most people.

Virtually no skill has been required. Anyone can pull the trigger; anyone can point his gun at a moving object, and pretty accurately too, before it gets into his shoulder, and even more accurately when it does get into his shoulder if he trusts himself, and does not try to 'make certain' or 'swing with it' or whatever he has been told.

And does not all the advice to 'shoot instinctively', 'squirt at 'em' and so on now fall into place? Of course it does.

It is *so* easy that it might be worth trying it with your gun in the garden on some small birds, with a pair of snap caps. These are dummy cartridges, designed to absorb the blow of the hammer. With an empty gun, the hammer blow might damage the breech face or the hammer itself. If you have shot for some years, it will at first feel unnatural to keep the gun with the bird all the time you are mounting. Persevere! And later this season, everyone will be commenting on your good shooting, smooth mounting, and the fact that you seem to have plenty of time!

Point or swing

If we are to go further, we must break down one or two prejudices. Nearly everyone I talk to agrees that 'swing is everything'. This includes the down-the-line expert, the average shooter, and (sometimes!) the good shot. But never, I submit, the 'class' shot. This is because swing is not everything. It is not necessary at all.

I keep on saying that shooting can be easy. It can indeed be so, if only we use the physical and mental attributes which we have all been given. It is because we do *not* use these assets that good shooting requires skill and thus can be difficult.

I repeat, all of us can point accurately and quickly. We cannot easily and instinctively swing any stick, gun or what have you in line with a moving object. It is comparatively difficult for us, and requires learning, patience and practice. Some have more skill at it than others; but virtually all – even the most skilful 'swingers' – are inferior to the 'pointer' in accuracy, solely because pointing accurately is instinctive.

And yet very few of us use our inherent pointing skill when shooting. Why not? It is because when we watch a good shot it *looks* as if he is swinging his gun. If he is a very good shot, he is in fact not swinging the gun at all: he is pointing it.

It would be quite possible to watch (and indeed photograph) two good shots taking, shall we say, a fairly high, fast pheasant. The mounting and firing of both men could well appear identical to the observer, and indeed later when comparing them in photographs. What would be quite different – and of course quite invisible – would be what is going on in each man's brain.

One man's brain is saying 'Point' all the time; the other's is saying 'Swing ahead of the bird, and keep on swinging.' It may well have taken the second man years to achieve the correct swinging motion of his gun; most probably it has taken the 'pointer' just a few minutes.

We learn by imitation. We can see a man 'swinging' smoothly, and so we try and imitate him by swinging likewise. Of course if he is not swinging but pointing, we are trying to imitate him the hard way. There is an unconscious rejection of pointing as people are loathe to disbelieve their very eyes!

It is basically for this reason that pheasant and partridge shots usually make such a hash of grouse shooting. You cannot swing at a grouse coming straight at you. You have not time to swing on the downwind grouse out to a flank, if you are to kill two in front. You *must* point at the bird and pull the trigger if you are to be a good grouse shot. And if that is true of grouse shooting, it must work for all other kinds of shooting. You cannot go through your shooting life with one technique for high pheasants, another for driven grouse, and yet a third for rabbits. If the pointing technique works for one, it must work for all.

Of course, nearly everybody does in fact swing; when they miss, they try to swing even more! It is difficult to unlearn your swing and start again the easy way. The easy way of pointing your gun has become difficult to put into practice every time, not because pointing has become hard, but solely because you have assiduously practised the mistake of swinging.

GUN
COACHING!

Point with the left forefinger

This is why the average small boy can so quickly become a good shot. He learns that pointing is the way to do it, finds he can do it easily, and thus, provided he is not told it just cannot be that easy, ends up as a 'class' shot.

One of the best ways to teach a newcomer to shoot is to tell him to lay down his gun and then, without the gun in his hands, to adopt the 'ready' position with his arms and hands, pretending to hold the gun. When the clay comes over, I tell him to point at the clay for as long as he can with his left forefinger (assuming he is shooting from his right shoulder).

(*opposite*) He learns that pointing is the way to do it

After doing this a couple of times, I ask him to pick up the gun. When it is loaded, I pat the barrels and say, 'That is your "finger".' The last boy who did this shot very well. His father was grateful, and was kind enough to add, 'What a beautiful swing he has now got.' You see what I mean!

It is a waste of time to practise an instinct
An author I know writes most intriguingly about newcomers learning to shoot. But at one point, he goes off the rails – at least *my* rails! 'Constant practice is the keynote to success,' he writes. I believe this is wrong. Many sports, and most certainly shooting, can be mastered quickly and certainly without the need for constant practice.

My belief is, and always has been, that if anything can be done very well by anyone, it must –indeed has to be – simple to perform. Shooting can be performed beautifully by quite a number of people. For this to be humanly possible, the process of shooting well must be simple. Even the best shot in the world is built very little differently from the rest of us – if at all.

At this stage, most readers will throw up their hands and say, 'If it's that easy, why is not everybody a good shot?' Why not indeed! The answer is elementary. We all know the natural golfer who arrives on the first tee with words to the effect that he has not hit a golf ball for over a year. His drive goes straight down the middle for over 250 yards. We who have been diligently practising hit the ball about two-thirds the distance (if we're lucky) and into the rough. The natural golfer is a single handicap player, and the others never will be: one is doing it the simple way, and the rest are not.

As I have said, if I ask you to 'point at the top of that tree' you will do it accurately. If you practise for twenty years, you will do it no better, because you did it right the first time. It is not necessary to practise an instinct. Virtually all of us can point accurately; virtually none of us use this attribute to make us good shots.

I have quoted the instruction to 'shoot instinctively' as the advice of our forefathers. On the face of it, what a fat-headed bit of advice. Yet were they perhaps not trying to tell us to *point* instead of *swing*, solely because the one way is instinctive and the other not, thus letting us down unless we practise? And some people practise for much of their lives without much result! Of course a lot of first-class shots do practise, and I am not saying that this is not useful. But basically they are practising their concentration, not their method – provided of course that their method is the easy one.

I have no doubt over-simplified things a bit to stress my point. There are clearly other facotrs such as the correct position of the gun in the cheek and shoulder, the master eye, good footwork and so on. But nearly all this falls into place as soon as you start pointing.

'It's easy, Dad!'

Your brain controls your shooting. As soon as you school your brain to issue simple easy instinctive instructions, your muscles will at once respond without continual practice. To this day, I can hear the comment of a small boy hitting his tenth clay running, off a high tower with his .410. 'It's easy, Dad!' Since Dad had previously announced that these particular 'birds' were out of shot for his 12-bore, you can understand why people are disinclined to believe what I say about it being easy!

Let me make my final point. There is a book which has a splendid photograph of a man shooting a clay from the hip. The caption says: 'A vivid demonstration that the hands alone can align a gun correctly. Surprisingly, the method calls for no more skill than is given to most of us . . .' Surely this then is a very good base on which to build all shooting instruction. There is no need to *fire* the gun from the hip – just mount the gun so that it *would* hit the target if you pulled the trigger at any point during the mounting.

The caption continues: '. . . but no novice should attempt to use it.' Why not? If it is 'surprisingly easy', why not? Here in the photograph is a demonstration of the truth – the easy key to all good shooting. The truth is being held upside down because no one – up to now – has realised that it is indeed the dead easy route to good shooting.

Imagine you have a bayonet on the end of the gun and try to push it into the bird as you are mounting

Of course, I am being rather unfair. It *would* be inadvisable for a complete novice to fire from the hip without appreciating the recoil unless the gun is pushed at the target, as of course it should be.

But, as I have said, the truth is there. Why hold it upside down? If it is easy – 'no more skill than is given to most of us' – then that method should surely be tried.

I quote from Churchill's classic *Game Shooting*:

> In the shooting school, we are often able to demonstrate this fact [that gun mounting is correct] to pupils in actual practice. When a pupil ... is missing ... we instruct him to pull the trigger on the word of command. As soon as a clay pigeon comes over, and before the gun is on the pupil's shoulder, we order him to fire ... With the gun in the half-mounted position, he finds again and again, he is shattering the clay. The lesson that that teaches is that if your eye is on the bird, and you are mounting correctly, you haven't got to worry about anything at all.

Yes, of course. But only 'if you are mounting correctly'. Not in a million years am I going to fire my gun from the half-mounted position *to see if my gun mounting is correct*. I might miss. Then what do I do about my gun mounting? Alter the whole thing and start again? It might go on for years.

No! Here again is the truth upside down. Turn it over, and it will read, 'Try to mount your gun so that it *will* hit the clay if you pull the trigger at any point during the mounting.' Try and do this; the nearer you get to this desirable state of affairs, the nearer you will get to becoming a really good shot. Let us go a little further. If we mount the gun with the bird for say one second, surely we shall be more accurate than the man who flings up his gun and has only about one-tenth of a second in which to aim and get the 'picture' right. Ten times as accurate? You are perhaps getting into the 'class' category right away!

As you can see, a number of people have had the key to good shooting for years. I have simply turned it round so that you can

'Try to mount the gun so that it will hit the bird if you pull the trigger at any point during the mounting': not very successful here!

use it. In the past the theory has been: 'If you hit the target whilst you are mounting the gun, *then* you are mounting the gun correctly.' I say: 'Mount the gun so that you *will* hit the target during the mounting of the gun, and *then* you will be a good shot.'

Positive instruction, and very easy to learn and carry out.

I believe that, as shooters limp towards the achievement of being good shots, nearly all instructors, whose job it is to cure the limp, are 'bandaging the wrong leg'. When teaching or writing on how to shoot, they firmly try to instil the correct 'picture' *when the gun is about to be fired.*

Let us see what happens. We are told, let us say, to 'rub the bird's feathers up the wrong way' and then fire. It works for two or three shots, and then we miss. If asked what happened, we say, 'It felt all wrong that time.' And of course it *was* all wrong. Why?

We are so anxious to get the 'pull-the-trigger picture' correct that we lug the gun up with a snatch. We never think that the mounting of the gun is of any importance. If we do not think about it – and if, in addition, it is seldom taught – we shall find the problem of getting the 'picture' right very difficult.

One example. Many of us mount ahead of the bird; if you do

Many of us mount ahead of the bird

this there is often not much 'connection' between the gun and the bird as the gun comes up. The gun is then unconsciously checked as the trigger is pulled, and you miss behind. You realise you were astern and next time mount further ahead, thus making quite certain that the gun will check, and you still miss behind. More lead as you mount, and eventually you hit because the gun is so far ahead that you hit by interception. This gives you a bit of confidence and next time you keep the gun moving. You are now all set to miss in front for the rest of your life!

I know what I am talking about. I may not be believed, but at least half the experienced shots that come for a lesson – 'Can't hit a thing – getting too old to keep up with them' – are consistently missing in front, solely because of bad gun mounting.

Let us make it easy! And it will become so if we bandage the correct leg for a change. Concentrate on the correct mounting of the gun, and make the whole thing fall into place. When you do it properly, the 'picture' is always there and correct as the gun comes into your shoulder. When I am teaching and I see the pupil mounting with the target and pulling the trigger as the gun comes into his shoulder, I do not bother to look at the clay. I know he will hit it, *and he always does!*

How to practise your gun mounting
Now how to mount your gun correctly with the target. First you can practise by yourself, so no one need know that you are trying out this heretical method.

Stand in front of a fairly tall looking-glass, and get the gun into the 'ready' position: that is, the butt tucked firmly between the right upper arm and the right side, and the gun roughly horizontal. Now imagine, say, a partridge flying straight towards you, level with your eye. If you then point the gun at the reflection of your right eye, you will be pointing at the 'partridge'.

Keeping the gun still at the 'ready' position, point the gun until you think it is pointing – from the hip so to speak – straight at the reflection of your eye. Now drop your eye down to the reflection of the muzzles and see if you can see two round holes at the end of the barrels – and *only* the two round holes of the barrels, and no part of the barrels themselves. If this is the case, the gun is pointing straight at your right eye – and of course at the imaginary partridge. If it is not, move the gun about until you can only see the two round holes of the end of the muzzles.

Now, keeping your eye on the two round holes, slowly mount the gun so that all the time you are mounting you can see only the ends of the barrels and not the barrels themselves. It is surprisingly easy! In about a couple of minutes you can do it quickly, and after a couple of sessions, you can do it very quickly – more quickly than you will ever need to when shooting. You will, in short, quickly get the feeling of mounting with the bird, although it is so far only a case of a bird coming straight at you.

Why not try it outdoors with a friend? Go on to the lawn, open your gun and show it to your partner empty. Then use *his* eye to mount the gun on, and get *him* to tell you whether you went high or low or whatever as you were mounting. When that works, get him to walk slowly across you, still looking at your muzzles. Mount on his eye as before. All this is easy to do, as we are using our inherent ability to point *at* anything.

You cannot deal with an overhead target like this, obviously, but if you get your friend to stand behind you, he will be able to say whether your gun was 'on' the starling, or whatever bird you selected, all the time you were mounting. You need not do it quickly; take your time. There is always more time than you think.

In future, when the gun comes up, the 'picture' will always be ready waiting for you. Almost instinctively you give the lead that is required. Remember that the gun is *on* as you mount, and then moving at the same speed as the bird; any lead must thus be an *acceleration*.

It really *is* simple to mount the gun as I suggest. But since you have, prior to this, probably been mounting (let us be polite) in a different fashion, you will revert when you go out shooting. You must therefore do a bit of practice in the mirror.

Correct mounting of the gun, with the bird all the time: obviously easier shooting

This is what the bird sees if you snatch the gun up, as in the second picture.
The gun is never with the bird

Skill or technique

My definition of a good shot is the man who shoots well when he is shooting badly. This is rather Irish, but everyone will know what I mean. Anybody can shoot well when he is on form. But to be a consistently good shot, we must have a sound and simple technique. With this, we shall never shoot really badly; we shall be good shots. I have learnt the art of good shooting by teaching, watching and coaching all sorts of shots – good, bad and dreadful, and I do assure you that I know how to shoot very well.

'How modest,' you will exclaim. 'Surely he is asking the Gods themselves to wreak vengeance on him for having the cheek to say that he is a good shot!'

I have said no such thing. 'Physician heal thyself' – how difficult that is. I know *how* to shoot very well. I do not say that I always do so. And so perhaps I am indeed ideally qualified to help other people discover why they are missing. To do the same for myself is quite a different matter.

Basically, when we miss, the reason must be either mental or physical. Get these two factors right and we shall never miss. Let us set about it.

The mental side is the most difficult to get right, because we all find it so difficult to know what we have got to do in order to hit a moving target. It is of course impossible to run through a 'cockpit drill' as the bird approaches. 'Stance – check position of feet; grip of left hand – fingers not on top; right hand – OK; head still' – and so on. You cannot possibly do it. You have got to have something simple that you can remind yourself of quickly. Equally vital, you must believe that this 'something' will, if correctly performed, ensure that you will always hit the target.

I repeat yet again: *pushing and pointing the gun at the target all the time you are mounting* is both easy to remember and inherently easy to do. What is more, it will, if correctly carried out, solve virtually all the technical problems of shooting. It will give you a sound technique. You must accept this; you must have faith in this simple truth. There is no other simple solution to the mental problem; and I can assure you that it works.

But most of us – virtually all of us – at once throw overboard any theory if it does not work immediately. If you do this you will never get the mental side right. Since you can only get the physical side right by doing correctly what you are mentally trying to do, you *must* get the mental side right before you go any further. And I believe the only way to do this is to get my simple theory into your head, so that you can physically carry it out. It is a theory that is both simple and correct; and if you accept it as correct, it will work.

Accept it for five shots anyway. Now try to carry it out. You have at least now got one leg firmly anchored before taking the next step. You now have to get the physical side right, and this is pretty easy – far easier than getting the mental side right.

You may accept this principle of mounting with the bird, but what does it feel like when you are doing it correctly? This will be difficult to describe because the feeling may be different for each person. I shall attempt to describe the action in a rather extreme way in order to get across what I am trying to tell you.

I mount the gun with both hands and arms pushing out towards the bird. With the gun thus pointing at the bird, I can maintain this position for as long as I like. I am looking at the bird. I am not conscious of the gun, although I know it is pointing at the bird. It is not yet mounted into shoulder and cheek.

When the bird is 'right', I complete the mounting of the gun with a sort of snap – after all, it has only an inch or two to go to get into the cheek and shoulder – and pull the trigger. The 'picture' is right as the gun fires. I am moving with the bird and can pick it off as I like. It gives complete confidence. Now you can do this mounting or 'holding the bird' for as long or as little time as you like, *provided you do it!*

I was coaching someone recently on high 'pheasants': he got the hang of the idea and literally held the bird for as long as three seconds before finally mounting the gun and shooting it (virtually overhead). I then suggested he could take them earlier, provided he 'held' the bird, even if he did the holding business for

When the bird is 'right', complete the mounting with a sort of snap and pull the trigger

a shorter time. Of course, he instantly reverted, mounted behind, pulled through and missed in front! So I made him go back to the previous leisurely style, except that I asked him to 'pull' when I told him to. As soon as I saw the gun with the bird, I said 'Pull!' He at once completed the mounting of the gun, 'pulled' and of course hit the bird.

Eventually, he seemed to be hitting the clay almost on the end of the trap. But to do this, he was indeed 'holding' the bird – though only for a short time – before he finally mounted and fired his gun.

The only reason you miss is because you do not push and point the gun at the target all the time you mount. Why do you fail to do this? Jacket too tight? Foot slipped? Too hurried? There is an easy solution to *these* mistakes.

Shoot like a boxer

I repeat that we must have *some* mental gimmick on which to base our shooting. There are of course dozens purveyed by friends, instructors, books and so on. Do you remember? 'Good footwork is everything', 'come up his smoke trail', 'pull through', and so on. But at least my advice of pushing and pointing looks possible. It would appear to be simple, and indeed will require little or no skill. This latter point is highly desirable.

When someone comes to me because he believes that my advice is good, but that 'it won't work for him', the answer is always the same. He is not doing what I advise, although he thinks he is. He is not pushing and pointing the gun at the bird all the time he is mounting it. He may have practised in the looking-glass but, in the excitement of shooting, he is failing.

It was a well-known shot who first said that the position adopted by the good shot before mounting his gun was that of a boxer. How right he is! Adopt it without a gun in your hands and see if it feels right. Then take up your gun, and hold the position. If you are left-handed, then the 'southpaw' stance is for you.

Now to shoot well, all you do is punch the target with the old-fashioned straight left. Your body goes forward slightly with the blow; your right hand comes forward too, to guard your chin; your head has not moved. You need not, indeed must not, do it very quickly as you would when boxing, but deliberately. I frequently find myself saying when coaching, 'Punch it on the nose.' After the shot I say, 'Now do it like that, only more deliberately.' And they are away.

(*left*) The beginner is trying to *aim*; not enough *push* towards the target. Note the use of a walkie-talkie to control the trapper (see Chapter 3)
(*right*) 'Shoot like a boxer': the good shot demonstrates. It looks right!

With this 'boxing' advice, you will be doing what I advocate – pushing and pointing at the target. Everything falls into position – the movement of the gun, the correct position of the body and head, and (of course!) correct footwork.

Trust the mounting of your gun
It is a curious human trait, which manifests itself very clearly in shooting, that the vast majority of people are convinced they are doing what you are advising, when they are not.

I used to lecture young officers in naval gunnery. They were, and still are (unless human nature has recently changed materially) an idle lot, but the subject sometimes was not without interest. At my best, with my audience with me and even laughing at my jokes, I reckoned that never more than 30 per cent of what I was saying was absorbed.

And so it is with this chapter. You may read it – even with interest perhaps – but unless I can jerk you awake, you will not get any benefit from what I am saying. Tchaikovsky realised this and deliberately woke his audience up with a bang in one of his symphonies. It is a sad illustration of human inattentiveness that you have actually to wake people up to listen to genius making music of sublime orchestration and invention, and when they have paid for it, too! But to face reality, all this is necessary if you are to get your message across. Here then is my shooting message:

Shut your eyes before you pull the trigger!

Please don't slam the page shut. There is a great deal of sense in what I am saying, if you will let me explain.

I am sometimes accused of being repetitive. I expect I am, but I try to say the same thing in different ways so that it gets through to different brains. If it reaches one person each time, surely it is worth it; and it boils down always to the same thing, because there is only one easy way of shooting very well.

Mount the gun with the bird, and when the gun comes into your cheek and shoulder, *all you have to do is to pull the trigger*. But people don't just pull the trigger! Their eye instinctively slips from the target to the gun to make sure that it is correctly aligned, because they cannot believe that the pushing and pointing when mounting the gun has done the job for them. They thus start aiming with the gun in their shoulder – often only for a moment and even unconsciously – and so they miss. The only time they do comply with my advice is when they fire a snap shot – and that is why they then so often succeed.

If you mount your gun correctly, and then shut your eyes (both eyes, of course!) before the gun is completely mounted and so before you pull the trigger, you just cannot correct or aim when the gun has reached your cheek and shoulder. All you can do is to pull the trigger. The first time I tried this when coaching a young man who was missing because he tried to 'correct', he hit the clay. After expressing extreme astonishment as to where it had gone, he never missed again.

By shutting his eyes before pulling the trigger, he simply *had* to rely on the correct mounting of the gun. He simply could not 'correct' for any imaginary errors, and so he hit the target again and again. The trouble is of course that so many of us do not mount our guns as I suggest we should. What most do is to bring up the gun any old how, as quickly as possible to allow more time to aim with it in the shoulder. (I believe this is the sole reason why there are not more than about six men in the whole of the UK who consistently shoot more game than they miss.) What closing your eyes does do is to correct a mistake which so many of us commit: although we mount our guns correctly, we do not have faith and pull the trigger.

I am of course not writing to deceive; I am leading up to another and more practical way of correcting this mistake. Look at the target, concentrate on the target, and take no notice of the gun. You should now find this easier to do, because you now know *why* you must do it.

Look at the bird, put your gun smoothly to it and pull whilst still looking at the bird.

Timing

I have coached fifty people at shotgun shooting in a day at a game fair. Nearly all were comparative beginners, though there were a number of 'experienced' shots amongst them. Every single one of them made it difficult for himself to shoot well, by making a mistake. And in every single case, it was the same mistake.

The mistake every man (and woman) made was to regard the business of mounting the gun as simply the process of getting the gun quickly into the shoulder and cheek – and *then* getting on with the business of 'aiming' and shooting.

We all say of a good shot that he seems to have plenty of time. And we are right: he does! How on earth does he achieve this, when we are doing a 'Wild West' mount: surely no man could do it quicker? We fall back on the well-known anodyne – he does it instinctively.

Now instinct is nothing but an excuse. When we use it of the activities of human beings or animals, it really means that we do not understand how it is done. When we say that racing pigeons return to their loft 'instinctively', it merely means we do not know how they do it. We do not say that a game dog follows a wounded pheasant instinctively, because we know it does it by scenting it: yet if we did not know about scent, we would readily use the word 'instinctive' about the gun dog.

So it is unhelpful to retreat behind that word 'instinctive'. What is it then that gives the good shot so much time? It is so unfair that a chap who is already a good shot should have more time than the duffer. Or perhaps it is *because* he has so much time that he is a good shot. Where, then, does all this time come from?

One factor is that 'getting it up quick' is *wasted time*. Such mounting of the gun does not contribute in any way to the accuracy of the shooting. And paradoxically, the quicker you 'get it up', the more time you will waste. The reason is that with this 'common-sense' mounting, the gun is not moving with the target. You have got to start the business of shooting *after* the gun is mounted.

I have coached fifty people at shotgun shooting in a day at game fairs

I have always said that you have more time than you think when shooting. But you have not got minutes, and to chuck away time when you need it must mean hurried shooting, the root cause of all shooting mistakes. The average shot mounts his gun very quickly – let us say it takes about half a second. He then spends at least a second – probably rather more – getting the gun on, giving the target lead, coming up its smoke trail or whatever else he thinks is necessary, and finally about a third of a second pulling the trigger. Probably over two seconds in all.

Before we finally come to the sensible answer, surely we can argue that often we could save time by starting earlier. If we stick to our 'gun up quickly' technique, this is merely going to leave us longer on aim with the gun in our shoulder – a worse example of poking as applied to shotgun shooting than we achieved before.

Surely the answer, as I continually advocate, is to mount the gun with the bird. Then, when the gun comes into the cheek and shoulder, not only will the 'picture' be correct, but the gun (and arms and body) will already be moving with the bird. Say one second for the mounting and a third of a second to pull the trigger. Nearly twice as quick – or, conversely, nearly twice the time you had when you mounted the gun in a hurry.

When I coached the beginners, I was continually asked where the clay had been missed. With hurried gun mounting, it was quite likely to be anywhere: the shooting was inconsistent. So it was no good telling the pupil that one shot was for example high, when with no correction the next shot would have been low. All I would have achieved by telling him 'high' would have been to cause the next shot to be lower still. And all this simply because every pupil was wasting time, and thus shooting inconsistently solely because he *had* to hurry.

Afterwards, someone came up to me and said that it was amazing how he could see everybody suddenly begin to hit them after a few minutes' instruction. The answer was that at last they had enough time. And that alone was why they started to become better shots. And it was only the careful 'with it' mounting of the gun that was making this possible.

Slow down

I want to emphasise what I am saying about saving time. 'An absence of haste is characteristic of the better performers.' I did not coin this rather pompous phrase myself, but it introduces one piece of advice that always works when the average shot starts missing: *slow down!*

It is very interesting to see the reaction of a reasonable man when offered this guidance. You can see him being – in his own mind – desperately deliberate, and obviously thinking that, though it is foolish, he had better give the idea a chance.

The result is always the same. First, he hits the bird. Second, he mounts more smoothly than before – though not much slower! And finally, in actual practice, he shoots the bird earlier.

Let us see what happens when the 'slow down' advice is taken. The gun is no longer mounted hastily, but is brought to the shoulder with more precision. If the 'gun' has any experience,

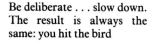

Be deliberate . . . slow down. The result is always the same: you hit the bird

there is, at the very least, a strong tendency for the weapon to be mounted with the bird, which is of course correct. Now, when it comes into the shoulder, the 'picture' is at once correct. All the 'gun' has to do is to pull the trigger.

The man who 'slows down' and hits the target asks, almost in self-defence, 'Wasn't I taking it very late?' I can always point out that, in actual fact, he has taken the bird considerably earlier. That settles it! At once, you have a potentially good shot on your hands.

The snag is that when you tell a man to slow down, he may interpret this to mean 'start mounting later'. This is a real difficulty because under these conditions there will obviously be less time to shoot the bird. I have seen 'guns' do this, who in all sincerity had no idea that this was what they were doing, when trying to comply with the 'slow down' instruction.

Finally, I am being absolutely truthful when I say that a more deliberate mounting for the man who is having a series of misses virtually always means hitting the bird, *and* shooting it earlier. It is this last fact that perhaps justifies your advice in his eyes. It is very largely because he shot the clay earlier – *not* because he hit it! – that your advice appears acceptable.

'Take your birds early'
Everyone who shoots knows this is the so-called acid test of the good shot. It is, in itself, good advice but it has saved the lives of countless head of game. It is a teaching that has a sort of snob value. 'So-and-so is a brilliant shot: he takes his birds so early.' How often do we hear that?

And we try to do likewise. The obvious (and wrong) way to achieve this business of shooting your birds early is to hurry. We see a young 'gun' blazing away and missing consistently. If we asked his neighbour (aged seventy, and with practically every bird killed that he had shot at), the old boy would reply that at his age, he realised that it paid to take his time. And further, if you asked, say, a disinterested beater, he might well describe the old boy as a 'wonderful shot who shoots them quick', and the young man as someone 'who'll learn in time'.

By all means take your birds early, but do not hurry in your attempt to do so. If you hurry your gun mounting, you will take longer to get on your bird. You will, I assure you, be both quicker and more accurate if you mount your gun deliberately.

This is where we came in – the one piece of advice that always works. Slow down!

Relax

It is perhaps not often that a famous racing-car driver, or a destroyer captain, can be said to have any close connection with good shooting. But I believe that something can be learnt from any master of his trade.

Nuvolari was the Italian Grand Prix champion of the 1930s who always drove for Alfa Romeo. When he drove, he insisted on the knob of his gear lever being moulded in quite soft putty – for comfort, he said. At the end of the race, the putty was virtually the original shape, in spite of changing gear hundreds of times. If you think this nothing, imagine dropping two gears – no synchromesh! – at 120mph approaching a corner. If you missed the change you went on, in every sense of the phrase. What sort of a shape would your putty-headed gear lever be in after the race? And what on earth has this to do with shooting? Wait and we will see.

Changing the subject for a moment, there is a descriptive phrase invented by destroyer captains. They talked of a 'white-knuckle day'. Admirals used to have a habit of telling the destroyers which were screening a line of battleships on the starboard side to do it on the port side – and do it quickly. Now it is a bit tricky to go in between two 35,000-ton battleships doing 25 knots. More than one gallant officer has gripped the destroyer bridge rail very hard indeed during the cross passage, and hence the phrase.

When shooting it is very easy to get into a state of tension and though you know that you are in fact tense, you usually do not realise that your muscles are as taut as fiddle strings. Your mind you admit is tense – but nothing else. People who come to me for shooting coaching are often extremely tense to start with. If I tell them to relax, they laugh rather shame-facedly and remain tense. This is because they try to relax mentally, which is very difficult, whereas they should try to relax their muscles.

If you are strung up, it is impossible to shoot well. Your muscles will work in a jerky fashion. If this is so, you will be unable to push and point the gun smoothly at the bird. You will snatch and jerk the gun. You will have all the faults of the beginner who mounts his gun in a rush, and then searches round the target in a series of jerks. With the best will in the world, you will not be able to achieve good gun mounting if your muscles are tense.

At one shoot I went to, they always arranged 'comforts' after the second drive. 'Comforts' was by tradition a mixture of sloe gin and cherry brandy – filthy, of course, but it took the gleam out of many a knuckle. Now of course I am not suggesting that 'Dutch courage' is necessarily the answer to nerves. I am simply saying that nerves are a grave hindrance to good shooting – not because they inhibit the mind, but because they stiffen up the muscles.

Of course you may say that you never suffer from nerves. Well I do! Imagine being asked to a rather important shoot. You draw the best position at the first drive, and start off by missing the first three birds (sitters!) with both barrels. What shape would your fore-end be in after that, if it had been fashioned of putty? You see what I mean: destroyer captains would have nothing on you. Your knuckles would be gleaming like polished ivory.

This is all very well, but where is it leading us? You have got to relax, of course; everyone can see that. But tell that to the chap who has just expended his sixth cartridge into thin air. Mentally I believe it cannot be done.

So you must relax your muscles, and there is quite an easy way of doing this. Nuvolari, although driving his car flat out, was utterly relaxed, and because he was relaxed was able to drive fast and accurately. And I suspect he was able to relax his muscles solely because he had a gear lever with a putty knob, which he simply had to handle gently and smoothly. Why not take a leaf out of a master's book, and handle your gun as though it had a putty fore-end, and a stock made of soft Plasticine?

Gun fit

Most good English gunmakers insist that a perfectly fitting gun is essential. Americans, on the other hand, are often very good shots and almost never have their guns fitted to them.

Both cannot be right – and yet can they?

You will have heard of the very keen shot who lost the sight of his right eye. He immediately had a gun made with cross-eyed stock so that he could shoot from his right shoulder using his left eye. To any two-eyed person picking up the gun, it appeared to point anywhere but where he was looking. The instructor came along, and in front of an audience fired a few shots to see how the gun was going, at some 'high pheasant' clays. He hit every one. Naturally he was asked, 'How on earth—?' His reply was simple: 'Closed my right eye.'

The object of a well-fitting gun is to ensure that, when it is mounted correctly to your shoulder, it will then be pointing where you are looking and thus will shoot to that point. Ah, but 'mounted correctly' – there is the snag! What do we mean?

I would describe this as the gun being bedded well into the cheek, assuming that the head has not moved whilst the gun is being mounted, with the butt in the shoulder and not on the arm. But of course for 'fitting' to mean anything, the gun must be mounted exactly like this *every* time. And the vast majority of us do no such thing, although we often think we do.

We do not! The gun often does not come up to the shoulder; it often does not come into the cheek. Or it does come into the cheek, but we have moved our head to get it there. And so on *ad infinitum.*

To 'fit' a gun to such a man is patently a waste of time. Of course, we can be sure that it is roughly right – the approximate length of stock and so on. But before a gun can be 'fitted' and all the benefits obtained therefrom, we must learn the correct position of the gun in the shoulder. And this must be achieved every time – the slow deliberate shot, the snap shot, the curling grouse shot, the hare going away – every time, the gun must come up to the correct position, the same position.

(*left*) An English gun with cast-off allows the head to be kept still
(*right*) An American 'mass-produced' gun, with no cast-off, requires the head to be tilted

How then can this be correct for the Americans, who do not have their guns fitted? The answer is that the American has learnt to bring his gun up into the same position every time, and then has learnt to correct for any misfit by moving his head to make the necessary adjustment, or shooting slightly high or whatever. But this makes it slightly harder for him, and therefore breaks our rule that we must make things easier for ourselves. So, learn to mount correctly every time, and then a correctly fitted gun will make it easier for you.

All this will work only temporarily for a schoolboy, because a schoolboy is growing and changing physically. As a young boy grows, he is getting broader, and his arms are getting longer. This point is most important. Every holiday I see lots of young boys shooting with the same guns they had the holiday before. I know without looking that they will miss high, because their stock will be too short. And they always do!

You can see this quite easily – and it can easily be rectified – for as the young man mounts the gun, you will see a gap between the butt and his shoulder. He then has to pull it back to get it into his shoulder. The cure is either:

(a) To hold the gun with his left hand (assuming that he is shooting from his right shoulder) further towards the end of the barrels; or

(b) To fit a rubber pad on the end of the stock. This is not always wholly satisfactory as the pad is sometimes inclined to wobble, and the rubber sometimes drags on clothing and prevents the butt coming right up. Since our philosophy is to make things as easy for ourselves as possible, think hard before you fit a rubber pad.

You will realise now that the position of the gun in your shoulder should ensure that your gun is pointing where you are looking without your having to correct it. Now, how to find out whether your gun-mounted position is correct for you? Mount the gun quickly, without aiming, at a prominent object, or a branch on the top of a hedge; then, keeping everything still except your arms, lower the gun until it is completely clear of your body. Are you now in a natural standing position, or is your head pushed forward and down? Put another way, do you normally walk about with your head in the position it was left in when you lowered your gun? If not, you are moving your head and making the gun come into the wrong position in your shoulder. You are not making things easier for yourself.

After shooting several shots, do you find a bruise the next

When the gun is into your shoulder correctly, it should be pointing where you are looking

If you find a bruise on the top of your arm, the butt was not into your cheek but out to the right on your arm

morning on the top of your arm? I frequently do, and it means that the butt was not into your cheek, but out to the right on your arm. If the butt was too far right, the barrels will be too far left, and you will tend to miss there.

Next time you pull your trigger, ask yourself, 'Is the gun really into my cheek?' Remember, it is possible to feel the bump of recoil on your cheek even though the gun was not there when it went off. What you have got to say to yourself is, 'The stock is into my cheek – bang – and I have kept it there.' You see, it is possible to put the stock into your cheek, then at the last moment unconsciously to lift your cheek off the stock (to see where you have missed?). And if you were subsequently asked whether the gun was into your cheek when you fired, you would be prepared to bet your life that it was. Do not: you would lose!

Finally, mount the gun at any prominent stationary object – chimney pot, branch, or anything you like. Mount it quickly without aiming, *keeping both eyes open*. Then, without moving the gun, squint along the barrels as if it were a rifle, and see where it is pointing. If on, you are all right. If you are out to the left of the target, read the section on the master eye in Chapter 2. If you are consistently high/low or otherwise off the target, the fit of your gun probably needs attention.

If you want gun fitting to benefit you, you must practise. Pick up your gun and mount it into the correct position in your shoulder and cheek five times every day. You can do it indoors, of course. Do it slowly, to make sure that your head is not moving. Do it quickly in front of a mirror to see how much your head *has* moved. Do it again quickly without moving your head.

I would summarise by saying that the 'fit' of a gun is desirable, but not vital. It depends so much on you, what you do and what you are.

How do most of us start? We buy a gun off the peg, and adjust our mounting position and head until we can hit reasonably consistently. This may be a 'wrong' or uncomfortable position, but that is the price we pay for not having our gun fitted. But provided we achieve this same gun-mounted position every time we shoot, we will shoot just as well as the 'gun-fitted' man.

If we then went to a gun-fitting expert, he would either leave our gun-mounted position as it is – in which case he would not need to alter our gun – or he would insist on a 'correct' position, alter our gun accordingly, and then we would have to learn to mount the gun into a new position and do it consistently.

Mount the gun quickly. Are you in
a natural standing position . . .

WRONG

or is your head pushed
forward and down?

Let us look at the chap being fitted. Assume for a moment that he has a gun that clearly does *not* fit him, and also assume that he mounts the gun into the correct (and same) position when he shoots. He will then miss either high or low, or right or left consistently, or, of course, a combination of these.

Now more or less cast – that is a sideways bend to the stock – will correct the right or left error, and more or less 'bend' – a vertical bend – will correct high or low. But evil things can befall the shooter who has an ill-fitting gun and poor gun mounting. Let us assume that the weapon has a bit too much bend. Now, if we mount the gun by mistake higher in the cheek, we shall quite probably find that all we can see from the right eye will be the top lever (the lever that opens the gun); and thus inevitably we shall not be able to see with this eye the bird at which we are shooting. But we shall continue to see it with the left eye, a fact which we shall not appreciate at the time. We are shooting with a completely master left eye, and we shall miss left by quite a bit.

This I am quite sure is one reason why we suddenly get an off day, especially at low birds such as driven grouse. We are virtually trying to shoot with our master eye shut!

It can happen to anyone. Gun fitting will not necessarily cure it: it is basically our fault. It is caused by mounting the gun too high in our cheek, by dipping our head down to meet the stock, or possibly by too much bend. Or, of course, by all these mistakes at the same time.

After all this, there is still the problem of correcting any right or left error of your gun and you. When a shotgun is mounted, the rib – the joint between the barrels – is a little to the right of the eye if the stock is dead straight, and this must theoretically be allowed for. But it is not much – try to see it in a mirror. And people's faces are much the same in broad physical dimensions. No! The reason for more or less cast-off is, I believe, the relative dominance of the eyes.

Thus a man with a dominant right eye – shooting from his right shoulder of course – would need very little or no cast-off. A man with a completely dominant left eye would need a lot: so much, in fact, that it would then become a cross-eyed stock. Clearly there are an infinite number of variations in between, but it does, I maintain, depend on the dominance of the eyes, and very little on any physical characteristic.

The object of gun fitting is to ensure that the gun points where you are looking without your having to aim. When being fitted, I have been told to fire at a plate. If I mounted the gun carefully, it was difficult not to aim at the stationary 'partridge' when it appeared: if I threw the gun up and fired without aiming, it was fairly unlikely that the gun was mounted correctly.

By aiming, you can pull the gun from quite a long way off the bird so that you will hit it, if you have the time. I have seen this 'aiming to get on' so often when coaching that I know how frequently it occurs. But it is to obviate just this that you have your gun fitted, and I am sure from my limited experience of being fitted that not enough technical equipment is available to exclude the 'aiming' which gets into the gun-fitting session.

In short, I would like to see gun fitting done 'backwards'. The stock of the try-gun would be adjusted in the shooter's gun-mounted position, until it was really comfortable for him, and correctly mounted. A lot of time and trouble would be taken over this, with insistence that the gun must every time be mounted into this position.

There would be no barrels on the try-gun, but merely a fore-end for the shooter to hold. He thus could not aim, but with the stock in his cheek and shoulder would be told to point with his left hand at a mark a few yards away.

A torch – adjustable for elevation and training and fixed out of sight of the shooter where the barrels would normally be – would be switched on when the trigger was pressed, and would show just where the shot would then go relative to the mark. The torch, when switched off, would be adjusted until the spot of light was dead on when the trigger was pressed. When this had been achieved, the barrels would be fitted to align with the measurements achieved by the adjustment of the torch. The gun would then shoot where it was pointed.

Make sure the gun does come into your cheek and shoulder

Make sure that the gun does come into your shoulder. I wish to emphasise this. It is surely simple to say that one's eye is the shotgun backsight. But it is true, although one does not always think of things like that. If one does accept this fact, surely there are some interesting deductions to be drawn, all of which will affect the accuracy of the shooter. In short, it explains forcibly two points that I have already mentioned. And these two points are:

(a) You must mount the gun into the same place in your shoulder every time.
(b) You must keep your head still whilst mounting the gun.

If you break either (or both) of these two rules, you are obviously moving your backsight. And any rifle shot will tell you that this does not make for consistent accuracy.

And even if you do comply with these two rules, your gun even then may not be 'zeroed up' correctly. In other words, when your gun is mounted consistently and your head is not moving in the process, still you may miss. You will, of course, then miss in a consistent fashion – by which I mean in the same place, as well as every time! Again, this is recognised in rifle shooting, where a recruit's rifle, for example, is zeroed up. This is a fairly simple process. First the recruit is told to fire – with his rifle rested (i.e. correctly mounted, with his head still) – at the bull on a target not too far away. The resultant group of say five shots is then 'moved' to the centre of the bull by the armourer pushing the foresight up or down, right or left, as required. If the group is a small one, then at the next attempt the rifle should be bang on. If the recruit shoots badly and has a large group, it is patently very difficult to tell where and how much to 'move' it.

We have no movable foresight on a shotgun, but the way a shotgun is zeroed up is by fitting the gun to the user. Instead of moving the foresight, as on a rifle, the stock of the shotgun is adjusted until the gun does point where the shooter is looking – at least in theory.

What we are saying is that, broadly speaking, a gun that feels comfortable, and is not corrected for a 'wrong' master eye, will shoot near enough where one thinks one is pointing it. And so it will – except for the major snag that where you *think* you are pointing it is not where the gun will finally shoot if you are moving your 'backsight' when you mount badly, or moving your head and thus altering it drastically. You are the same as the bad rifle shot who produces such a large group that it can never be brought bang on – and even if it were, the margin of error from shot to shot would still cause a miss. Having got your stock comfortable, take great care that you do not move your 'backsight' all over the place every time you put the gun to your shoulder.

Now doesn't this begin to strike home? Last Saturday, you were obviously a bit underneath, and finished the day rather well by shooting 'up to them'. This Saturday, you unwittingly move your head down a bit as you mount, and then by shooting up to them contrive to miss over the top. It takes all morning to realise you are now shooting high. And by shooting straight at them, you manage to kill the last four birds. And so on – *ad infinitum!*

Of course it is the blasted gun – anyone can see that! It *must* be! Except that, of course, as always, it is *you!* Do not take this last sentence too lightly. I have done this so often, to my own disadvantage, that I now take great care. I know, for instance, that I do not move my head: I have told so many people not to, when coaching them. Nevertheless I had not been shooting too well the other day and, with the aid of a few clays, was trying to find out why. Whilst waiting for the clay, I could feel my neck resting lightly against my collar. After the shot – I hit the clay rather with the edge of the pattern – I suddenly realised that I could no longer feel the collar.

Had I pushed my head forward and down? Surely not! But next time, I deliberately kept my neck against my collar, and the clay dissolved! Ten shots later, again I began to hit the clays with the edge of the pattern. What was wrong now? It just could not be my head moving *this* time. But of course it was! I had forgotten, like so many before me; and exactly as you will, whatever your resolution, unless you practise.

I have watched a film of Percy Stanbury taking a few clays. Of course, he never misses. But when you see this film, do not watch the clays, for this is a waste of time. Watch his head. It looks as if it had been clamped in a vice!

After all, the down-the-line boys do not miss very often. If you come to think of it, they have got their backsight pretty well fixed for every shot, because they have plenty of time to make quite sure that this is indeed so. So can you with a bit of practice, even when shooting at live game. And when you do, why should you also not kill four birds out of five – and that is better than virtually every game shot in action today.

Not much footwork here – and clearly he is going to miss

Footwork

Good footwork is not vital to successful shooting. Think of the wildfowler stuck in the mud; he has not got any footwork. The rough shooter in roots – not much footwork there.

But we are back to our old cry. 'Let us do everything we possibly can to make shooting easier for ourselves.' Good footwork will help you; where you cannot move your feet effectively, then you will have to do without the help that good footwork can give. But do not let us do without it unless we must.

You should stand with your feet quite close together, and they should be placed at an angle of about 45° to your right. Let us just see why this is correct.

Your feet should be quite close together – your heels, say, about 9in to 1ft apart. The reason for this is to enable you to pivot easily with the weight on one foot. If your feet are a long way apart, you will find it difficult to pivot, because both feet tend then to remain flat-footed on the ground. Pivoting to right or left then depends solely on the flexibility of the hips, and not all of us have any hips visibly and flexibly left. We are thus not making it easy for ourselves if the feet are too far apart.

70

I have two shooting books, one of which says categorically that for a high pheasant, the weight should be on the left foot; and the other book says on the right foot. Both cannot be right – surely? But I think they can! We can translate both 'rules' as meaning weight on *one* foot, *not* on both. This makes sense to me, and I think it will to you. I have said that the feet must be close together. It is then easy to transfer the weight on to one foot, and this is what you must do.

Now the other premise that I put forward was that the feet should be pointing at about 45° to your right. There are obviously two extremes from this: one with the feet 'sideways', that is in the army stand-at-ease position, and the other with the feet one in front of the other. There are pretty heavy disadvantages with both extremes, which we can avoid with our 45° compromise.

Let us see. Stand with your feet 'sideways' to your front, as if 'standing at ease'. Now raise both arms in front of you; if you are holding a gun, so much the better. You *must* lean back to counteract the weight of your arms and gun, or you will fall flat on your face.

To lean back and shoot from off your heels makes shooting very difficult for you. You cannot turn or pivot. In fact, if you have read this book at all, you will see that I am advocating pushing the gun towards the bird all the time. If you push the gun forward, your body must follow. And so it should. With a low bird, this means leaning forward; and this is impossible without falling over if your feet are 'sideways'. With a high bird, pushing the gun at the bird as you mount means reaching up, and even this is difficult with the sideways stance if the bird is in front of you at all. So *not* sideways.

The other extreme is with the left foot in front of the other. And more people get into this position than they realise. (Do you? Of course not . . . but have a look, all the same.) If you do do this, it will then tend to push your left shoulder towards a bird coming from your front – and, more important, your right shoulder away from such a bird. Now as you mount at the bird in front,

71

Your feet should be quite close together to enable you to pivot easily with the weight on one foot

your cheek will tend to push the butt outwards, so that with the right shoulder back, the butt mounts on the top of your right arm, and not in your shoulder. You will miss – and 'unaccountably', too!

Now the weight on one foot. If you stand with the weight on your left foot, your left leg and body can become an upright shaft about which your body can rotate easily. 'Easily' is the operative word – make it easy for yourself. You can then swing right or left, upwards or downwards, always able to push the gun at the bird as you mount. Your weight will be on *one* foot, and so you can turn easily. If you prefer to move your weight on to the right foot for a bird on your right, there is no objection, but the weight must be mostly on *one* foot.

This means that you are always leaning towards the 'bird' when you are shooting – that is, leaning down and forward at rabbits, forward at, say, low-flying grouse, and reaching up towards the high bird. All this follows from the instruction to push the gun at the bird when you are mounting. And this is correct. You must not overdo it, of course; there is obviously a limit as to how far forward you can lean at a low bird in front of you. But this caveat does not alter the principle I am trying to instil.

There are psychological factors working against this. As you mount your gun, your instinct is to lean back to counteract the weight. Good footwork will counteract this. When a fast low bird comes at you, it is quite difficult psychologically to push the gun and yourself towards it. Yet you must. Your footwork must allow you to. It is, after all, difficult enough to overcome the instincts which will tend to make you mount your gun wrongly. Do not make it well-nigh impossible with bad footwork.

2 Firing Your Gun

Lead or forward allowance

It is an incontrovertible fact that lead or forward allowance is required in order to hit a moving bird. The amount of lead depends on several factors, but mainly on the speed of the bird and the angle to you at which it is flying.

In short, the gun has to be ahead of the target, to a greater or lesser degree, when the trigger is pulled – or, to be more pedantically accurate, when the shot leaves the barrel. The necessary lead will look different to each person. If two people are firing at the same bird from the same position and kill it, the actual lead given by them will be the same, obviously. But *one* may say he gave it 6ft; the other may think he gave it only a few inches. What is the correct lead is utterly immaterial here; what concerns us is what the correct lead will look like to you.

That the correct lead does look different to different people is true, I am sure. I will go so far as to say that the correct lead so far as one person is concerned may well seem to vary from day to day. Have you ever noticed how, at the end of one day, you were killing birds with comparatively little lead, whereas at the beginning of the next day out you are clearly behind with what looks like the same lead, and have to give more?

The answer is not a corroded liver, or a thick night the night before. *It is in how you mount your gun.* If you mount your gun correctly, the apparent lead you have to give will not vary for you, from day to day, or hour to hour, or ever.

If you read the section on gun mounting, you will see that you should always achieve an accelerating swing by mounting the gun with the bird, and then almost instinctively going slightly ahead as – and *not after* – the gun comes into cheek and shoulder. With an accelerating swing, the apparent lead always

74

seems a good deal less than when you achieve a swing that is, unknown to you, slowing down.

In fact, when mounting correctly, for fast birds fairly close to, you appear to need no lead at all. Close to? Why? When the bird is close to, you are moving your gun quickly if you are with the bird as you mount, and so unconsciously give the correct lead as you *apparently* shoot straight at it.

Thus when you start mounting correctly, and giving the same lead you used to when you were mounting the gun badly, you will tend to miss in front. If the close and fast birds can be shot by apparently pointing straight at them, this makes it easy for you.

But some lead *is* required for the really high bird, and the bird a long way out. Remember, *you must mount with the bird – not ahead* – and as, and only as, the gun comes into cheek and shoulder can the gun be moved fractionally ahead and the trigger pulled.

Take care not to mount ahead of the bird, because then there will be no acceleration to the swing. Mount with and at the bird. Take care to see that any lead is smoothly 'added' *as* the gun comes into your cheek and shoulder. Take care not to give too much lead. If you are mounting well, as you have been taught, the lead becomes a minor factor; it *feels* like a few inches. The whole thing is being made easier for you.

Aiming or pointing
Now nearly all the questions that you are about to ask boil down to the fact that you think you will not be able to understand how pointing and shooting *at* a moving target can possibly work. May I go back to the bicycle-riding analogy for a moment? Everyone knows that it is possible to ride such a machine; very few know why, but this does not stop them riding off on two wheels with complete assurance. If you asked them, they would all say 'balance', and yet there cannot be much balance about it or you could stay upright on a stationary machine. If I explained to my small son, before he started to learn, that a rotating wheel behaved like a gyro which stays upright in space, I do not believe

it would help him at all. The same will apply to virtually everyone if I try to explain why mounting and shooting at the moving target works so successfully. May I suggest that to have confidence in what I am saying about shooting is all the battle.

For the simple, and apparently illogical, method that I advocate does in fact work, and works for every kind of shot, too. I was a naval gunnery specialist, and so knew all about aim-off at aircraft. The British invented an ingenious sight which automatically gave the correct aim-off, and it worked by pointing the sight continuously *at* the aircraft – all done by gyros, incidentally. I wonder if we have the equivalent of gyros – normally used to make it possible for us to stand upright – which enable us to work out the fairly complicated geometric problem required to hit a moving target? Idiotic and far-fetched, of course, but undoubtedly we have some calculating mechanism. Everybody has, for I have coached more than fifty people in a day, and everyone who could point the gun at the clay while he mounted it hit the target if he had trust and 'pulled' without making sure.

In actual fact, I believe that anybody pointing at a moving object points ahead of it unconsciously because he feels that his finger must actually point at where the object will be by the time his reaction has been taken into account. To achieve this, however, he must *point*. He must not aim or align his finger on the moving object.

When I photographed racing cars by simply pointing the camera at the car, I always got a picture of the front wheels only. The speed of light was faster than No 7 shot, so I 'missed ahead'. Thus, when not using the viewfinder (aiming!), I had pointed ahead without knowing it. Now I reckon that the lag of the brain which causes us to point ahead of a moving object helps a very great deal with the lead required when using a shotgun. You must however point and not aim, if you are to take advantage of this ability common to us all.

What is the difference between aiming and pointing? I believe that the answer to this question is one that goes far towards solving the difficulty of shooting well. Aiming involves seeing the gun barrels, and thus (you think) being able to adjust their point of aim to align the gun on the target. This is the snag, for the vision of the gun has a very strong effect on the eye. The gun is moving only because the gunner's eye is on the target: if he sees the gun, some part of his vision at least has left the bird. Take the eye away from the target even momentarily, and the gun will tend to stop, because there is then not much incentive to keep it moving. Aiming must involve seeing the gun. The man who aims has to give a lot of lead, because as soon as he gets the gun 'on', it begins to slow down. All sorts of dodges are thought up to overcome this self-imposed difficulty – 'pull through it', 'come up his smoke trail', and so on – all designed to counteract the slowing down of the gun caused solely by aiming.

I say that when good shooting is easily achieved, it is all in the mounting, and nothing in the aiming. I do not say aiming is wrong. Many people can shoot well that way, but I believe it requires a good deal of practice and skill to overcome the inherent disadvantages. Why not use a method that has inherent advantages. Very little skill is required.

The human factor
Let us suppose that the lead as laid down by the mathematicians for a fairly fast partridge 30yd away is 3ft. It is important to realise that this is the distance that the barrels must point ahead of the partridge *when the shot comes out of the gun*. This is often not what happens, even though the distance ahead may have been correct when the decision to shoot was taken. You can frequently see this: look at the 'guns' on your right and left actually shooting. Often, it is quite clear from the angle of the gun relative to the bird that the weapon was actually pointing *behind* the bird when fired.

If you went up to the chap afterwards with some tactful remark about 'pretty quick birds', you would doubtless get a reply to the effect that he knew all that, that he gave them plenty of lead and even that was not enough.

Could you then tell him the truth? That is:

(a) The lead he initially gave by mounting the gun in front was too much; and
(b) Because the gun stopped moving with the bird, it was in fact pointing behind it when the shot came out, lead or no lead.

He would not believe (a), and he knows as an experienced shot that he does not 'check his swing', so he does not believe (b) either. What does he do? The 'gun', who is completely unaware that the way he has mounted the gun gives him a strong tendency to slow it down relative to the bird, does the obvious thing. He increases the lead, and begins to hit them! But he will not be consistent; he cannot be. He has introduced two errors – the 'slowing down' swing and the 'wrong' lead – and it is against the laws of chance alone that the one will always cancel out the other. And if one or the other (or both) goes wrong he is in a mess, and goes to an instructor saying that his shooting is getting no better, indeed even worse.

Frequently I have coached a fairly experienced shot who, although mounting badly, does hit the first two or three clays. As I have already told him that I am going to try to teach him to shoot correctly, and not simply to hit the clays, he is not too astonished when I tell him that 'that will not do'. After I have explained my everlasting theory about mounting with the bird, he gets it, and I shout, 'That's it: that's the way we do it!' The pupil turns round and says, 'But I missed.' My next words, as night follows day, are: 'Mount just like you did then, and shoot straight at it.' The clay disintegrates.

The pupil turns to me and says, 'It is just not poss——' and then we both burst out laughing. Not only is it possible, but he has just *done* it. You can see what has happened: the 'gun' has mounted his weapon correctly, and then the first time has given the same lead as he has 'learnt' to do when mounting the gun badly. And he misses in front. This happens so often when I am coaching that I suppose I should anticipate the error. But I think it is quite a good thing to let it happen, as this impresses the pupil more than mere words. In short, the man who is using two mistakes to hit the bird must eliminate both of them if he is to become a consistently good shot.

Now the reader can very well say that we have had an awful sweat to learn a new way of mounting the gun, simply to learn a different lead from what was sometimes 'correct' before. Well, I suppose that is one way of putting it. But what we *have* done is virtually to eliminate lead in our mind's eye for most of our shooting, and reduced it to reasonable proportions for the very high or very long shot. Virtually at his beak all the time.

The really high bird
That is all very well, you will say, but of course it will not work for the long 'crosser', or the very high bird. I was out shooting the other day when I heard my next-door 'gun' shout, 'Oh! Why pick on me when you know jolly well I can't hit them when they come as high as that!' He was utterly unaware that he had even opened his mouth, but sure enough there was a very high cock pheasant coming straight for him. And sure enough too, the bird took not the remotest notice of either barrel that greeted him. He sailed on with that indefinable air of the bird that clearly has not even realised that he has been shot at.

Not all of us blurt out our feelings as a high pheasant approaches, but this chap who unconsciously did so undoubtedly voiced the thoughts of many of us. 'Why pick on me! You know I can't hit them as high as that.' Haven't we all felt that?

But if they are in shot, why are they so difficult? Some people can hit them and bring them down stone dead again and again. To preserve our ego, we are told that the 'gun' in question has merely got the knack of the high bird, and probably could not hit a bolting rabbit to save his life. This does perhaps help those who cannot hit the 'archangels', but not much, because we suspect it is not quite true.

Not many high pheasants are really out of shot. Owing to

some quirk in our visual equipment, a bird 40yd overhead looks half the size of a low bird the same distance away. And the average gun will be annoyed if he misses the low bird, and often will not even fire at the bird overhead if it is over 25yd up.

A high pheasant does indeed look small, and this I believe is what makes it seem so difficult. There seems to be no 'connection' between the gun and the bird: firing at it merely becomes a mental salute, with the gun pointed upwards, stationary and probably vaguely a long way in front. It would be fairly difficult to achieve a more faulty technique.

A high pheasant does indeed look small ... but not many pheasants are really out of shot

The bird will be a long way up by the time it reaches the trees where the 'guns' are

How then are we going to hit them consistently? We must stick to our system, remembering that the easiest way to shoot is to point the gun at the bird all the time you are mounting. To mount the gun with the bird, you must look at the bird and not the gun. Concentrate on the bird.

Let me give another explanation of mounting with the bird. I mean that the gun must be mounted 'all of a piece'. There is a strong tendency, with the high bird, for the right hand to pull the butt up to get it into your cheek and shoulder: down will go the barrels, and you have to catch the bird up again. One hand is mounting faster than the other.

Both hands must mount the gun together. If you mount with one hand faster than the other, the gun will see-saw as it comes up and so it will not be with the bird when it is being mounted. I repeat that the mounting of the gun before it comes into the shoulder and cheek is the vital part. I do *not* mean putting the gun into your shoulder and then keeping it on the bird like a rifle.

If your gun is moving with the high pheasant as you mount the gun into the shoulder and cheek, the pheasant will be stationary relative to the gun. In short, you have turned a difficult shot into literally a 'sitter'. And we all know a sitter is so easy that it is unsporting to shoot at it! If you mount your gun as I say, this is just what it feels like as the gun comes up.

Now I am quite sure that if some high birds are missed behind, an equal number are missed in front. I do not like talking about lead for a bird, and I only do so now to point out where I believe people go wrong.

I have always maintained that the amount of lead that you should give is what it looks like to you. It may in fact be, say, 6ft, but it may well look to you like 6in. If the bird looks tiny because it is a long way up, the lead – even if you work it out mathematically as, say, 6ft – will even then look small. And if you mount the gun correctly with the bird, the correct lead to hit will look to you comparatively small, too. If now you follow my advice with the gun moving with the bird and thus feeling as if it is pointing at an apparently stationary bird, you can simply point your gun just in front as you pull the trigger. And this is how lead is given.

And I do assure you that this 'mounting with the bird' business does indeed make all the difference to your shooting. If you do it correctly, you really do seem, as the gun comes into your shoulder and cheek, to have it pointing at a stationary bird, and you can pick him off as you like. Both bird and gun are moving, of course, but relative to each other they are indeed stationary.

Finally, trust your gun. There is no need for long barrels, full choke, high-velocity cartridges or large shot. The length of barrel will make no material difference to the velocity of the shot, and the boring of any length of barrel, like for like, will throw identical patterns.

You know that No 7 shot has sufficient blow up to 45yd, and you know that a full cylinder will give you a dense enough pattern at this range. So, mount with the bird, and trust your No 7 cartridges.

82

Poking

Poking is a word that is used frequently in shooting. The act itself has probably saved more lives of game than any other.

We all know that poking is wrong; in fact, it is considered 'bad form' to be guilty of it. It is the dirty word of shooting. Everybody, almost instinctively, does what he can to avoid being accused of this sin. And yet nearly everybody does it to a greater or lesser degree.

Let us see what poking really is. It is aiming with the gun already mounted into the cheek and shoulder. In a bad case, a 'gun' will mount his weapon quickly, and then spend quite a long time aiming at the bird in order to make sure that he will hit it. This is poking. Now, if you come to think of it, anybody who aims his gun after mounting it badly has to do just this – either quickly or slowly – in order to correct his aim.

So severe is his fear of an accusation of poking that a 'gun' will do anything to escape it. And often the only way that he can see of avoiding it is to do everything as quickly as possible. How often have we heard somebody say that he can hit birds that come quickly at him, whereas the birds coming from a long way off present, to him, an insuperable problem? (In fact, I have heard of some 'guns' who, seeing a high pheasant coming, will actually look at the ground until they judge the bird to be roughly above them, and will then snap at it as it comes overhead.)

Basically, all this is to avoid being accused of poking. If they had never heard of the word, they would mount the gun any old how, and then correct the aim, slowly or quickly, according to the speed of the bird. Although they would, in fact, be guilty of poking – as they are now – they would be slightly more accurate shots than the man who, determined to avoid the accusation, snatches the gun up quickly and fires in a hurry.

There is another phrase which should be remembered in this connection, and that is 'take your birds early'. This phrase has caused almost as many misses as the fear of poking. In effect, the average 'gun' trying to obey this 'commandment' does exactly the same as when he is trying to avoid poking. He snatches the gun to his shoulder, and, having made that mistake, shoots quickly. But if you mount with the bird, and shoot when the gun gets to your cheek and shoulder, you will *easily* be able to take your bird early.

You will see at once too that the instruction to 'fire as the gun comes into your shoulder' automatically prevents poking, or indeed ever being accused of it, however deliberately you are shooting. But we must remember that it is absolutely no good firing as the gun comes into the cheek and shoulder, *unless you have mounted with the bird.*

All of us who mount in a hurry, any old how, are therefore nearly always guilty of poking because we have to correct our inaccurate aim *after* the gun has got to the shoulder. By definition, this is poking. The more we try to correct this by shooting quickly, the more inaccurate becomes our shooting. If we mount the gun with a quick snatch, or even if we mount the gun slowly without mounting it with the bird, then we are in trouble.

Be humble! Say to yourself, 'Am I poking to a greater or lesser degree?' If you are not mounting the gun with the bird and shooting as the gun comes to your shoulder, you are, indeed, poking – with all the attendant evils thereof.

Special shots

A sound system or method of shooting must work for all types of shot. I am not sure you are convinced! You will say that the method advocated in this book will not 'work' for some particular type of shot. (The type of shot where it will, in your opinion, fail will of course differ for each reader.) It *will* work. It will always work, if you do it correctly.

'But what about the———?' You fill in the gap with the shot for which you think it will fail – high pheasant, going-away shot, snap shot – what you will. In order to reassure you, I propose to deal with a few of the different types of target, so that I may make it quite clear that a sound system will *always* work.

Snap shot

Let us suppose that you are shooting driven grouse, and a bird suddenly appears towards your right when you are looking towards your left. 'You have only time to lift up your gun and fire,' you will say. This is of course just not true. I will suggest that if you have time to 'lift up your gun', you will have time (as an alternative) to push the gun instinctively *at* the bird and fire. In this latter case you will of course kill it, for this is the method I advocate. You have to do it quickly, though unhurriedly, but this does not alter the fundamental correctness of it.

Point *at* the bird, and pull. In this case, that is all there is to it. If you *lift* the gun up, it will be a fluke if you are 'with' it; it will be a fluke if you hit it.

I keep on saying 'unhurriedly'. Common sense suggests that if you are short of time, you must do something 'quickly'. Yes, of course; but you must also be unhurried, for, strange as it may seem, this will make you both more accurate and *faster*.

I remember an officer in one naval ship in which I served. He was in charge of a batch of young officers, and was very keen that they should beat the sailors at a skill in which sailors were considered untouchable experts. At this time, there was a murderous contraption known as a '6in loader' which simulated the loading and firing of a 6in gun, with its 100lb projectiles. The navy, being what it was, used to run 6in loader competitions, competed for with great determination by all ships, and which incidentally greatly improved the gunnery of the fleet.

The young officers gradually improved their skill with early morning practice, and got their time for ten rounds down to 52 seconds, which was very good. The navy record was approximately 50 seconds. To achieve a 52-second time, the young officers were of course flat out, lifting and ramming the heavy shells through the contraption in a mad rush. The 'drill' had become pretty instinctive by then.

The officer then said – inspiration, did he but know it – 'Let's try an unhurried run.' The time was 48 seconds! They eventually got down to 46·5 seconds, and this time has never been beaten, and never will be.

Make haste unhurriedly. Misquoted and trite – but how true! When you are out shooting, you have more time than you think. Be unhurried – always.

Going-away shot
How often do we hurry this shot. The bird is flying away, and soon will be out of shot. The gun is flung up – bang! bang! The bird flies on, still leaving time for another shot, and probably two. Put the gun smoothly *to* the bird, look at the bird, and 'pull' as the gun gets into the cheek and shoulder.

When a bird is flying away from you, there is inevitably a tendency to aim the gun as if it was a rifle. You can *only* do this by adjusting the aim after the gun has got into the cheek and shoulder. This is *wrong*. It is not possible to aim, in the accepted sense, if you fire as the gun comes into your cheek and shoulder. If I insist on your firing immediately the gun is mounted, which I do, then the inevitable tendency to snatch the gun to your shoulder – you have little time, you think – will cause you to miss.

Let me repeat: smoothly with the bird, look at the bird, and 'pull' as the gun comes up to cheek and shoulder. It *seems* slow at first to you. It is *not!* Everybody else will be saying that you always seem to have plenty of time.

High pheasant
Remember a really high bird is a difficult bird for anyone to hit. Make sure your technique is perfect, with the gun correctly mounted in your cheek and shoulder. If you are slightly wrong, you will miss. Why not practise this? Mount your empty gun in the garden at a bird overhead; as it comes into your cheek and shoulder, stop! Then, keeping the gun where it is, come down with the gun still mounted in your cheek and shoulder until the

gun is horizontal. Are you in the correct position for a low shot? Head not moved? Gun into the shoulder and cheek perfectly? If not, you are going to miss your high birds. If all is well, you will kill them consistently.

Finally, do not be scared – at least try not to be – by the anticipation of the bird coming straight for you, getting higher and higher. I repeat: use the time he gives you. Do not leave it until the last moment before mounting and try to make it into a snap shot; you are making it harder for yourself if you do.

Long crossing shot
Have you noticed how the moon, when newly risen and close to the horizon, looks much larger than when it is high in the sky? It is, of course, the same size; but it *looks* bigger.

In the same way, a bird near the ground looks bigger than when it is high up. This has two effects. A high bird looks higher than it is, and a low bird closer than it is. You will thus tend to miss the long low crossing shot behind, because the long shot does require some forward allowance in your mind's eye.

There is a very strong tendency at these long crossers to throw the gun up well ahead of the bird and pull the trigger. In this case, you may take it for granted – I have seen it so often – that the gun is quite stationary on firing. In other words you are trying to intercept. The forward allowance *then* necessary is the distance the bird flies whilst the shot is getting there, *plus* the distance the bird flies during the time elapsing between your brain saying 'Fire!' and the shot getting out of the barrel. This latter time is longer than the first, and will also vary from day to day, even shot to shot.

In such a case, to hit is practically impossible. You are not getting an accelerating swing, or even a slowing-down one. You are getting none at all!

Mount with the bird, push the gun *at* him, and then, as it comes into cheek and shoulder, go in front of him. A little further than usual – the moon is 'bigger' low down.

When you push and point the gun at the target, your gun will point at that target if your right eye is the master eye

If the left eye is the master eye, the gun will point to the left of the target, and by quite a large margin

The master eye

One of your eyes is usually 'stronger' than the other. I have put the word 'stronger' in inverted commas, because I believe that 'stronger' does not necessarily mean better. I have always believed that one uses one eye more than the other, quite unconsciously, in much the same way as one is left- or right-handed, or left- or right-footed.

The fact that one uses one eye more than the other only becomes noticeable in shotgun shooting, where the gun is fired from one side of the body, and where both eyes are normally kept open. Sometimes a difficulty does arise.

Assuming that you shoot from the right shoulder and that the right eye is the master eye, when you push and point the gun at the target, your gun will point at that target. If the left eye is the master eye, the gun will point to the left of the target, and by quite a large amount. The explanation of this is best shown by a sketch, and I think the accompanying picture makes it clear.

As you will be unconscious of a left master eye – except by shooting badly – it is wise to check which is your master eye. There are at least two ways of doing this. One is to stand with your gun at the 'ready' position in front of a mirror, and then, keeping both eyes open, mount your gun, without aiming it like a rifle, at your right eye – that is, the eye over the stock in the mirror. Now, without moving the gun, squint along the barrels, and see if it *is* pointing at your right eye. If it is, all is well. If it is pointing out to the left, it may be that your left eye is the master eye.

Perhaps a better way is to try with a friend. Open your unloaded gun, ask your friend to walk away about ten yards, face you and put his finger up in front of his right eye. Now, show him the empty chambers of your gun, close it and come to the 'ready' position. Mount your gun, without aiming, at his finger. If all is well, your friend will see the barrels pointing straight at his finger and eye. If he sees your barrels pointing out to his right, with the end of the barrels aligned with your left eye, then you have a left master eye, and something must be done about it.

It is quite possible, as you mount the gun, for your friend to see the barrels start to go to his right and then come round to his finger and eye as you unconsciously correct. This may mean that you are *inclined* to be left-eyed. This, in turn, may mean that your left eye will take over in the case of birds to your left (and only then), or when you get tired.

89

We now appear to be in a hopelessly incurable state, but fortunately it is not so.

The easiest cure is simply to close the left eye! You must close it – or wink it just sufficiently to allow the other eye to take over – early on, as soon as you see the bird. If you leave it too late, you will start mounting with the left eye in control, and as a result with the gun to the left of your target; then, as you close your left eye, you will realise this, and have to correct. Close the left eye early, and you will be able to mount correctly with the bird.

If you are truly left-eyed, and do not like the idea of closing your left eye, you can instead:

(a) Shoot from your left shoulder, with a gun with cast-*on* instead of cast-*off*.

(b) Have a cross-eyed stock built. These are ugly and expensive.

Closing your left eye is certainly the simplest and cheapest solution, but it has snags. First, you lose the slight advantage of having two eyes – so far as shooting is concerned, not very bothersome. Second, you forget! You will have to practise closing your left eye, and we all know how difficult it is to practise anything. Indeed, it is quite a mental effort to close your eye to start with. I was once coaching someone, and told him to close his left eye, but he continued to miss left. I asked him if he was closing his eye, and he said he was, so I slipped round to his left and looked as he fired. He was doing no such thing – his left eye was wide open all the time. (I then made certain that he did close his left eye, but his shooting got slightly worse, and I found that he was now closing *both* eyes!)

But closing or winking the left eye early on is the complete cure. You will inevitably forget to do it at first; remember this fact, and it will help.

It will help a great deal more if you practise closing your left eye when you practise mounting. Is that too much to ask? I fear so!

Spectacles and shooting

How many medical experts can define the master eye? Of course we all know what it is – the stronger eye, the better eye – all very simple. But I believe that this definition is wrong. It is not necessarily the better eye or the stronger eye. It is usually one eye which by practise or habit has become the dominant eye.

Talk about splitting hairs! As if it mattered. But it does matter, and matter very much on occasion. It may be the cause of a young man 'never quite getting the hang of it', or an older man 'going to pieces' so far as his shooting is concerned.

We have all read that the master eye can change with age or even with practice. But what most people do not think about is the possibility that – apart from an accident of course – it may change quite suddenly, and indeed frequently, even several times a day.

I recently coached a man of over seventy whose shooting had 'gone to pieces', but who had been a good shot. Sure enough, despite a complete (and understandable) lack of confidence, he mounted his gun well, and pulled the trigger 'in time' with the bird. But he hit only a few clays because most of his shots were out to the left. But, not all of them! Now here was a problem.

He was wearing glasses, and said he had to for shooting because his right eye was so blind that he could see very little with it. It was at once clear that his left eye had taken over, and this was causing him to miss left. Easy! So I suggested he close his left eye when the clay came over, and then he missed right for the next half-dozen shots. Back to square one.

Open both eyes again, I suggested, and we had the usual miss-to-the-right, miss-to-the-left procedure, with the old boy practically weeping – and me too! We had a stand-easy to think things out. Then – inspiration! I told him to take off his glasses. He said he would not do that because he could not see much with his right eye, and he would be 'all over the shop' if he wasn't wearing his 'specs'. He could not have been worse off *with* them, so I gently insisted and he took them off.

He had one shot when he missed in front, and then did not

91

miss another clay. His 'dud' right eye, out of which he truly could see very little, was his master eye – and the spectacles designed to make life visible were confusing the dominant eye.

Much the same thing happened to a friend of mine who was also teaching. He confirmed that his pupil was right-eyed, and off they went. Steady misses to the left, with occasional hits thrown in just to encourage and confuse. It was then noticed that the 'gun' was wearing sunglasses, and he was asked if he needed them. 'Oh, yes: they correct my left eye which is not very good.' 'Try taking them off.' Well, you know as well as I do what happened then, and the pupil was advised not to wear those particular glasses for shooting again.

Now these are only two cases, so statistically they do not mean very much; but one pair of glasses designed to improve the vision of a master eye actually *reduced* its dominance, while another pair designed to improve the vision of a non-dominant eye *increased* the dominance of that eye. There are many morals to be drawn from all this, the obvious one being that not enough oculists take up shooting as a sport. But if you wear glasses – especially if you wear them for shooting – it might be worth checking to see that all is well. It is very simple. Get a friend to come with you and then, wearing glasses as you would for shooting, keep both eyes open and point with your left hand and forefinger at any bird that you see flying by. Your friend, if he stands behind you, will be able to see at once whether your finger is in fact pointing dead at the bird. Try at birds on your left and your right. If it is pointing correctly, then your missing is not the oculist's fault. If your finger does in fact point to the right or left of the bird, you can then perhaps blame someone else for your bad shooting!

See the shot

The idea that anybody can actually see shot fired from a shotgun travelling through the air strikes the majority of us as incredible. And yet it can be done, and in fact is being done pretty well every day throughout the year.

92

How else could the shotgun coach advise his pupil what that pupil was doing wrong, unless he could see the shot in the air?

'Oh well,' you say, 'You are talking about an expert, who has done this sort of thing all his life. They must have eyes like hawks.'

This is not true. Anyone, young or old, with reasonable eyesight, can learn to see the shot quite easily. There is of course one important proviso, which I will come to in a minute. But subject to this proviso, the ability to see this phenomenon can be acquired readily and can be incredibly useful.

I have a son who has been taught to see the shot. If he comes loading for me, it is of enormous help if he can tell me with absolute certainty where I have missed. (Provided he does not start to tell me *why* I missed, all is well!) It is an enormous help – almost unfair – and yet no one ever thinks of having his loader/companion, or whatever, taught how to see the shot. Of course the loader is there to load: he cannot always watch your shot *and* load. Bear this in mind in a hot corner when he says he 'didn't see', in answer to your frantic shout for help.

The proviso mentioned above is that you can seldom see your own shot. The reason is that, as the shot emerges, there is an appreciable flash, and this prevents your sighting the shot. This flash may not be noticeable by day, but it is only too apparent at night. In spite of this, I have in fact seen my own shot on several occasions. The reason probably is that the gun butt was so far away from my cheek – and the gun as a result pointing nowhere near the target – that I could see round the flash.

Once I had a bit of luck. I was in the 'hot' corner, and the first pheasant came well out on my left. I fired and the bird took no notice: I could see why. My shot was 3ft behind and 1ft high. In a flash I knew what I was doing wrong, and after that I had a terrific drive. That was indeed a fluke, but it would have been just as helpful if someone standing with me had given me the same information.

Now how to see the shot. The first absolute essential is not to flinch at the bang. Of course you don't: you have been out

shooting for years, and the thought is laughable. But you do – ever so slightly, and this is enough. Watch someone shooting, and he nearly always blinks slightly at the bang. Quite unknowingly his eyes are probably closing – or closed! – as the shot leaves the barrel. Cultivate the mentality of the shooting instructor who has reached the stage where each discharge bearly registers.

Stand fairly close behind the 'gun', and try to get into such a position that his mounted weapon is roughly in line with your eye. It cannot be, of course, and your eye will have to be above the line of the gun, and clear of the obstructing flash. Look firmly at the target – we will assume it is a clay, as a clay pigeon shoot is as good a place as any to learn – and, if you do not blink, you will see the shot as a dark blur, going incredibly quickly. If it hits the clay you will probably not see the shot in the air, but it does not then matter! With practice, the shot can be seen quite clearly every time and, as you acquire the knack, from practically any position behind the gun.

On crossing shots, the dark blur of the pattern will appear to curve away behind the target. This is an optical illusion, and will be clearly remembered by anyone who fired aircraft tracer in the last war.

If you miss the blur, you can very often tell where the shot missed by the 'feel' of the gun as the shooter mounts it. You can often see that he is starting, say, left of the target, keeping it there as he mounts, and finally missing there. On another occasion you may 'feel' him mount badly and then try to catch up with a frantic flick ahead, and duly miss in front. It is remarkably easy to shoot well when you are standing behind the chap who is actually shooting.

The spectator sees more of the game. This can indeed be most true of the sport about which we are talking. But nearly everyone is convinced that he cannot see the shot, or believes that only a

(*opposite*) The idea that anybody can actually see shot fired from a shotgun strikes the majority of us as simply incredible

chosen few can do it, and so he does not even try.

It is most helpful to you as a 'gun' if you can get reliable advice as to where your shot is going. Your spectator companion can so easily learn. In fact, he is more than halfway there if he reads this chapter.

3 How To Practise

The value of practising

I long ago came to the conclusion that when people are
frightened or excited, they act instinctively. I was training a
turret crew in a cruiser in the war. I knew this human reaction to
be true, so I decided that every day we would go through turret
drill – loading, aiming and so on – so that the crew's reactions
would become instinctive.

After a bit, someone said he could do it with his eyes shut. So I
thought we would try. We turned all the lights out, and went to
drill in pitch darkness. (This was quite something, as anyone
who has had anything to do with large naval guns will know.)
But the result was what we wanted, for when we went into action
– and all men are then both excited and frightened – the turret
crew found it difficult to do anything wrong. The 'drill' went
well, the gun was loaded and fired expertly, yet the turret crew
were scarcely aware to start with of what they were doing. They
reacted instinctively.

You will be excited to some degree when you are shooting, and
thus to some extent – more than you think – you will react
instinctively. If you dare, ask someone after a real 'hot' corner
whether he was, for example, mounting his gun correctly every
time – making sure of it. He will reply 'Yes,' if he is a liar; or, if
he tells the truth, he will say 'No. I did not think of it; I had not
time.' He had not time. Nor will *you* have time, and so you will
do it wrong unless you have practised until it becomes
instinctive. And this applies to all of us.

The really good shots often go to the shooting school – not, in
their case, to learn how to shoot, but to practise. This may be an
ideal way to do it, but it is not possible as a regular habit for most
of us.

Fortunately, we are all able to practise the various shooting movements quite easily whilst in our rooms at home, or even whilst in the office or waiting for a bus. I have more than once been brought back to earth with a bump, following a hissed whisper of 'Driven grouse' from my wife in church during a hymn, to realise that I had been practising my footwork, 'weight well forward on the left foot, pivoting easily'. I must have been taking them well out in front, beyond the vicar, for it to have been noticed!

Some movements cannot be practised indoors. Mounting the gun the way I suggest is one such movement. But this you can do in the garden, mounting 'dry' at small birds.

There are, after all, very few movements in shooting. They are basically:

(a) Correct footwork.
(b) Correct mounting of the gun.
(c) Correct position of gun in the shoulder.
(d) Correct moment of pulling the trigger.

Get these right by practising so that you carry out the movements instinctively without thinking. Then and only then will you perform them correctly, for you will find you will not have time to think when you are actually out shooting. You will be excited – at least I hope so – and will react instinctively. Will the reaction be correct? Only if it is instinctively correct, and this can only be achieved by practising.

You will realise that, for a beginner, this practice will have quick results. It is quite easy to groove your mind into the correct course. If you are older, and have shot for a bit, you will instinctively react in the bad old way if you do not practise the new correct style. And what is worse, you may even think that you are doing it correctly, while actually doing it wrong in the excitement of the moment. The result is instantaneous: 'This way is no ——— good, and the chap who told me wants his brain examining.'

It seems scarcely credible that, when you think you are actually carrying out a movement correctly, in fact you are doing no such thing. The truth is that in the excitement of the moment, you forget.

Let me prove this point. When I am coaching a pupil who, let us assume, is not putting the gun properly into his cheek, I will say to him, 'Gun into the cheek,' call for the bird, and he will shoot it. I can do this three or four times, each time reminding him about the gun coming into his cheek, and he will do it correctly. When I think he has got it, I will call for a bird without reminding him about his cheek and the gun. In nearly every case he will mount as he used to, incorrectly, with the gun not into his cheek, miss it, and then turn round and ask, 'What on earth did I do wrong?' He forgot, because he was not reminded. The answer is practice.

All the practice required to perfect your shooting is simple. Most of it really can be done anywhere – even in church! The best practice of the lot of course is shooting at live game, the next best is clay pigeon practice, and the last is 'dry' practice as advocated in this chapter, and which is very effective.

Without practice of some sort, you will not be putting into effect what you are trying to learn. I will go further. Without practice, you will *never* become a good shot – whatever books you read. *With* practice and intelligent guidance, you *will* become a good shot. It is as simple as that.

They tell you that shooting would be so boring if you never missed. On the contrary! If you used to miss, and tomorrow started shooting brilliantly, I am sure you would not be bored, even if you pretended to be.

After all, we do not go shooting hoping that we will fail to connect, although we may expect to. We hope to shoot well, and we are trying our level best to do so. How can it be boring to achieve what we are trying to do – especially when it is something that can be fairly difficult anyway? I am sure that people who tell you they would be bored at perfection are simply using it as an excuse. They know that they cannot manage it, and so chuck in their hand and do not even try.

Men and women practise their talents at golf, or playing the piano or other skills, but very seldom at shooting. The clay pigeon shooter does certainly, and I believe that a good skeet or sporting clay shot would prove a revelation to most game shooters if he was let loose at a big formal shoot. He would have to get over his nerves, of course, because a 'posh' shoot can be pretty intimidating to a newcomer. But with all these disadvantages, the expert clay shoot would not miss much: and anyone who could hold a candle to him would be in the top flight as a game shot.

You can almost hear the comments from the others: 'How boring always to shoot as well as that!' Untrue, surely, when in actual fact he is having the time of his life. Why do we go shooting, if we know we are going to miss frequently – and, worse still, perhaps wound? We try to hide behind any excuse. For instance, it is considered, they say, not 'fair' to practise. Success to be admired must be achieved 'naturally'; we all think more of the man who is a 'natural' good shot. How illogical: he has probably practised like mad, only we do not know that he has done so.

The truth is that we are lazy. 'But I go every year to a first-class instructor,' you will hear. Exactly! Why every year? Surely the *method* of shooting well can be learnt in one, perhaps two, sessions, and probably a good deal less. Why does one have to go again and again? The answer is regrettably simple: no attempt whatever has been made to practise what has been taught. And when you go back to the instructor the next year, the probability is that he will be aware of the mistakes you are going to make, because you made them the year before. He knows jolly well that you will not have made the remotest effort to correct them. It seems to me good for the gun trade, but a pure waste of money for the individual.

If we go to an instructor because we are not shooting well, and we leave him after an hour's instruction hitting them regularly, we must be doing *something* different. The difference, which is no doubt in our minds – in a pretty tentative way, did we but know it – is then not used until about a month later.

' Our unschooled muscles then simply do not obey the instructions our brain sends out, although we think that they do. The result is of course a miss, and because there is no instructor there to soothe us with good advice, serious doubts arise in our minds as to the infallibility of the instructions we have received. Two misses later, we are back on our own, using our faulty technique, and never getting any better.

'I think I'm missing those birds underneath.' How often do you hear that sort of excuse? I have used the phrase myself time without number, except it is sometimes 'over the top'; or, when things are very black, 'consistently left – my eyes must be going'.

Well you may be 'underneath' for one shot, but if you are doing it all wrong, the chances are that without any correction you will be over the top with the next shot anyway. If you believe the 'underneath' excuse is valid, your next shot will then be miles over. You are now all set for a pretty depressing day!

You have got to break yourself of the bad habits that you have consistently grooved into your brain and muscles over the years. However brilliant your brain, and however deep your mental understanding of the easiest method of shooting, you will revert in moments of excitement to your bad old ways unless you practise the new. You have no need to work at the new to learn the new, but rather to eliminate the old. I do not see any way of achieving this except by repeating the new easy methods. It *is* easy, but you have got to convince your muscles, which may be far gone in sin, of this fact.

After all, you can practise the correct mounting of the gun in your bedroom, say three or four times every day. This will take about one minute every week, and although as a busy man you naturally cannot afford the time, nevertheless it might just be worth trying!

Clay pigeon shooting

You may remember that I suggested earlier that the best way to practise, after shooting at game, was to shoot at clay pigeons. There are various ways of doing this, and the most obvious is to join a clay pigeon club.

Some time ago, I thought I would go one better, and *start* a clay pigeon club. It has prospered for sixteen years, and some of our ideas are unique. The object of the club is to improve our shooting. We now have one member who shoots for England, and where we have entered a team for WAGBI (Wildfowl Association of Great Britain and Ireland) or game fair shoots, we have either won or come second. Most of the team had virtually never fired a shot until they joined the club. We have had a great deal of fun, and our shooting has improved out of all knowledge. As it is so easy, I venture to tell you now how we set about it.

There were three or four of us who were keen to improve our shooting, and so we met to discuss what we should do. And of course the outcome was to form our own club. Here let me make two points. One is that there is no other clay pigeon club close to; and the other is that we decided from the outset that our object was to improve our game or sporting shooting. We have not gone in for down-the-line shooting. I mention this so that you will understand that our thinking is along 'sporting' lines, and that this has influenced our set-up, equipment and so on.

Having decided to go ahead, we looked round for a suitable site, and we found it under 2ft of snow in the winter of 1962–3. We approached the owner, the tenant and the occupier, and they had no objection to our using the site. This consisted of a large field; the only building was a farmhouse about 250yd away in one corner, and in the middle was a disused quarry. It was this latter feature that decided us, as it made possible high driven 'birds'.

We had another meeting, and duly elected a chairman, secretary, treasurer and committee. With the help of the Clay Pigeon Association, we drew up our rules, and these are printed as an appendix. They are self-explanatory, except for 'temporary membership', rule 25. This was inserted so that schoolboys could join during their holidays. We have not found it necessary to amend these rules, so they must work!

Finance

We charge £4 entrance fee, and £4 per year subscription. We amend these fees in the light of common sense if a member is elected near the end of the financial year.

Since we can buy cartridges and clays in bulk, we can effect quite a large saving for members. We sell them cartridges at a few pence per hundred above what they cost us. Clays we charge at 4p each, which is what they cost us to buy. It is the pick-up of the missed clays at the end of the day that helps to make this profitable.

Layout

Although we now have quite an elaborate layout, this came gradually. At first, your set-up will be simple; slowly you will be able to expand with your own ideas and enthusiasm. What I tell you now is really to show you ways you may follow if it suits your club. There are many other ideas.

High tower. Two of our members built a high tower of four telegraph poles, crossbraced with two platforms. This they did in one day, and it cost us nothing. We were lucky.

We enclosed a portion at the bottom of the tower, and this makes an ideal store-room.

We have two international type traps mounted at the top of the tower, and these throw the clays over the quarry. The quarry is about 40ft deep, and the tower traps about 30ft high, so the clays are about 25yd vertically overhead.

At first sight, they *look* impossible to hit, but in fact they can be consistently 'killed' with a ·410.

Grouse butt. We dug an ordinary butt outside one side of the quarry, and 'fired' the clays from a mobile trap on the other side. This is virtually a level shot coming towards, but of course at different angles and heights. Some protection was arranged for the trapper.

Partridge drive. The same members who built the high tower also arranged for bases on to which various traps could be quickly bolted. These bases consisted of large oil drums filled with cement, sunk slightly into the ground, with bolts grouted into the top. Mounting a trap is then merely a matter of placing the trap on the bolts, putting on the nuts and tightening up. We have put these bases in odd places as we thought necessary; all except one, which turned out to be in a useless position, are used regularly.

Probably the most popular position is at the head of the quarry, out of sight of anyone standing in the quarry. The clays come over quickly at a height of about 30–40ft, and the angle can be varied quite considerably.

Going-away shot. This can be arranged from any of the mountings. If a longer shot is required, we have a shield which will protect the trapper when the 'gun' wishes to go well back behind the trap.

Springing teal. Another member built a steel attachment which bolts on to one of the concrete bases, and on to which the trap is, in its turn, bolted. This cocks the trap up at about 60–70°. The trapper is protected by the 'going-away' shield.

Mobile trap. We purchased a foot-pedal trap by Bowman. This has been invaluable; it is a bit heavy to move around, but two men can carry it easily. It requires little effort to 'fire' it – by foot of course – and it is very quick. It is possible to get up to seven clays in the air at once, and the velocity, angle and height of the clay can be quickly and easily adjusted. The trapper sits! We had a bit of trouble with one of the ratchets, but the answer is never to fire the trap without a clay in it. The service offered by Bowman is first-class and cheap.

Walkie-talkies. I have long felt that shouting and whistling for clays to be thrown is out of date. If you are going to go in for driven game practice, the trap is inevitably some way from the gun and often out of sight.

So we bought two walkie-talkies for a total of about £120, and obtained the necessary licences. Apart from whip aerials getting broken, and batteries running out, they are still working well after ten years. They only weigh a pound or two each.

They are of course an enormous help. The trapper can be told what to do, and can of course communicate with the 'gun' when required. It is quite unnecessary to make any sound when the coach or 'gun' wants the clay to be thrown; if the 'transmit' button is pressed, this makes a 'plop' and a hiss in the trapper's receiver, and this is quite enough to tell him to let a clay go.

Walkie-talkies are not necessary for down-the-line, going-away and springing teal shots, since the gun is close to the trapper and a verbal call is quite sufficient.

Coaching

The object of our clay pigeon club, as I have said, is to improve the shooting of the members. Unless you have someone in the club who is a first-class coach, members will improve their shooting but slowly, and will often reach a 'ceiling' well below the standard of marksmanship of which they may be capable.

As virtually none of our members could afford to go to a first-class coach in London (surely the best in the world), we decided that he might be able to come to us.

Rex Gage of Holland & Holland has now been to coach our members many times. We are very lucky to have him: he is the kind of man who 'gives out' generously all the time. We arranged that he should coach our members in pairs for an hour at a time: in this way, starting at 8 am and finishing at 6 pm, with an hour for lunch, we could get through about eighteen members a day.

Other members of the club trap on a voluntary basis and generally help with clays, collecting empty cartridge cases and so on. The cost per member is fixed at £3, and any difference in the total is made up by the club.

As a result of this coaching, our shooting has improved out of all knowledge. I would like to see some of the club's better shots, who have never shot anything bigger than a pigeon live, out on a big pheasant day. Their standard of marksmanship would be an eye-opener to the average 'good shot'.

Schoolboys

I am a great believer in teaching sport to the young. They are keen, quick and responsive. To achieve this, we try to include a number of schoolboys among those to be coached by Rex Gage. We also organise schoolboys' matches, and we have a schoolboy cup to be competed for.

We have found that, under the spur of competition, the standard is extremely high, and we have to make the competition difficult. We thought at first that the very young, armed with a ·410, would need a plus handicap to even them up with their 'bigger' competitors. Never again! Most of the ·410 shots were getting over the 'possible' when the handicap was added in.

Club days

In the summer, we shoot twice a week in the evenings. Wednesday is a 'club night'. One of the members works out the programme, and there is usually a small sweep. The 'duty officer' rigs all the traps, arranges the programme and scoring and trapping and so on; the whole evening is his responsibility. On Thursday there is a coaching evening when anybody can come up to be taught, or to practise a shot difficult to him.

In the winter, we have the same programme on Sundays, arranged in morning and afternoon sessions.

And after all this, my advice is that if you cannot start a club of your own, you should join one. It makes your shooting easier for you.

Then and now

I have always thought that the Edwardian era was the age when sporting shooting achieved its highest point. There was a good deal of shooting available; the rich had infinite leisure in which to shoot and a practically infinite income on which to indulge their interest, while the not-so-rich had not enough money to shoot at all. Thus in general, shoots tended to be bigger and better than they are today, and those who shot did so more frequently and sometimes became more skilled.

Indeed there were several men who became such good shots that they were in great demand by those who had a shoot to 'establish', and by gamekeepers who wanted a good bag to establish *them*. There are many stories of their prowess.

On one occasion Lord Walsingham and Lord Ripon were next to each other at a drive waiting for the pheasants to come. Suddenly a covey of eight partridges flicked over the hedge between them. They got the lot! This story was told at the time not to emphasise in any way what good shots they were, but to explain how skilful they must have been to know which bird was theirs and which that of their neighbour. I have a feeling that most of us, together with any neighbour we liked to name, would be lucky if we got more than three between us.

It is frequently said to me that people who shoot as much as that ought to be good. But grouse flew no differently in those days, partridges no slower, and pheasants certainly no lower – in fact, almost certainly higher where that could be contrived. Their shooting technique must have been perfect. But remember, if they could do it, so can we. We also tend to remember the *good* old days. Not all good shots were as good as that; not all drives were so well conducted; not everything went better than today. As now, so then. Human nature does not change. With some men it was never their fault that they missed. (In those days, then two people had a bad day: that sort of gun and his loader.) With other men, it did not seem to matter; the ironic fact was that this sort did not seem to shoot badly very often. Or perhaps they did, and no one heard about it.

The fact is that the good shot in the Edwardian era was very good indeed. I have a feeling that there are few today who could approach him in skill. Why is this? The answer lies basically in one word – practice. You may remember that I have said that the best practice at shooting game is to shoot game. And some men had an awful lot of practice.

But the average shot of those days was almost certainly of a lower standard. What everybody lacked was anyone to teach him. Books on the subject were pretty hopeless; those who could shoot well did not know how they did it, certainly could not impart what knowledge they had, and were not particularly anxious to do so anyway. Thus those who could not shoot well and who were the least articulate were told to teach the young. The keeper was given the job of instruction.

I spent a long time with a keeper. I learnt a very great deal – not least what a great man he was. I wonder if employers realise what good service they receive from their keepers: and if they do, whether they do not take it for granted.

But he did not teach me to shoot. He could not. To start with, any skill he possessed was virtually confined to shooting vermin – on the ground. I do not suppose he could have hit one bird in ten up in the air. When I missed, he did not know where I had missed, and certainly not why. His job really boiled down to giving a young boy the opportunity to shoot at rabbits or pigeons. I learnt a lot about field craft and the country. But I did not learn how to shoot correctly. And this is how practically all present-day keen middle-aged shots 'learnt' to shoot. It was almost a fluke if they learnt the correct way.

It is different now. With clay pigeon clubs, there is opportunity for intensive practice, often under skilled supervision. If you practise under such conditions – in short if you are keen enough – you cannot fail to become a good shot, probably a very good shot. I am of course referring to sporting clays as opposed to down-the-line; nevertheless both help.

I have said it before, but I believe that among the best sporting shots in the country today is the good shot at sporting clays in an enthusiastic clay pigeon club. Almost always he gets no opportunity to show his skill at really difficult driven pheasants and grouse. But put him in a first-class shoot, calm his nerves by telling him that the man with the Rolls Royce and the pair of Purdeys probably has all his goods in the shop window, and he will outshoot everybody.

Perhaps another reason for the average standard of shooting being rather lower than today was the fact that the Edwardian in some cases – and I do repeat, in some cases only – liked to do himself well. I have two photographs to illustrate this.

One shows the 'guns' at lunch. This is obviously taken near the shoot, and is of course outdoors. Beside the seated 'guns' is a string orchestra of perhaps half a dozen players. The double bass looks particularly out of place in the open air. Although this may seem a bit odd, it is of course no worse than people who play their transistor radios in the open: but I maintain that both orchestra and transistor radio are out of place on the shooting field.

The other photograph shows a 'gun' with about twenty pheasants in the air. Behind him are two loaders and a boy. There is nothing particularly odd about this, but there is one further feature in the picture which strikes me as rather splendid – or the opposite, whichever way you look at it. On the ground to the left rear of the 'gun' clear of the loaders, is spread a cloth; on the cloth are three champagne bottles – two on their sides, empty, and one full. My only further comment is that the gentleman's footwork seems bereft of that easy fluency which no doubt characterised anyone who was good enough to shoot with three guns.

It can be said, therefore, that shooting skill is *on the whole* better than it used to be. It is still very bad! It is far below what could be achieved. A really good shot should kill and pick *consistently* more than he misses, and this without choosing his shots. Or, to put it another way (if you feel that 'percentage kills' are a bad way to judge a man's shooting), he should kill a great deal more than he does today.

The Edwardian age had its experts, who showed what could be done; if it could be achieved then, there are more opportunities now for more people to achieve that very high standard. There is a great deal of scope for improvement, although the average 'good shot' may be offended by being told so. Instead of taking umbrage – as I do, even when I am telling myself! – he should take steps to improve. It is easy.

If money in the Edwardian era was plentiful to some and taxation low, costs were in some cases not all that different from today. There used to be a saying about shooting a pheasant – 'Up gets a guinea, bang goes a penny halfpenny, and down comes half a crown.' I doubt if it costs a guinea to rear a pheasant even today. But it was certainly different with regard to guns. I am sure that the Edwardian period produced the best shotguns ever made – certainly in value for money.

A best London gun would cost about £65. A good example today of such a gun might cost ten times this amount; and it would be bought as a best gun to be used, and not for its 'antiquity' value. In other words, a best gun seventy years old would certainly compete with modern guns as to refinements, such as single trigger, ejection, easy opening and so on, and most certainly with regard to workmanship. But also, if it had been reasonably looked after, it could compare in longevity, even though it would have to give seventy years' start in this respect to its modern rivals.

There was intense competition to build a best gun, and I think there has been little improvement mechanically or in basic design since those days. This perfection was achieved because the skilled worker engaged on such guns gave his work unstintingly, with integrity and great dedication to the job in hand.

I can think of no other mechanical contrivance designed seventy years ago which can compete with its modern counterpart. When you consider that a best gun built seventy years ago can be very nearly as good a gun to use as its modern counterpart, you will realise what perfection of design and workmanship was achieved. Examine one, and see what I mean.

110

When I say that a modern best gun is as good as – or perhaps better than – an Edwardian best, I am giving the highest praise possible to the modern best gun. In view of the lure of the mass-produced cheap goods that can and very often *must* be bought today, there must be a strong temptation for even the best London gunmaker to skimp somewhere. The saving in expensive labour would be large.

There is no skimping. Perfection is sought to a degree which is almost incredible; the result is beautiful. There is here virtually no difference between *then* and *now* – just a bit better now to show that perfection itself is finality, and finality death.

4 Guns and Cartridges

Pattern and killing power

'Pattern fails before penetration.' This is a nice slick phrase which, spoken quickly, does not mean much to most people. The word 'penetration' is of course strictly inaccurate, and perhaps a better term would be 'killing power' or 'blow'.

What is meant really is that, *on average*, at the point where the pattern thrown by a shotgun fails, i.e. there are large enough gaps for the bird to fly through unharmed, the shot itself will still have enough velocity and weight to kill. Put another way, after the pattern has failed, killing depends on luck.

Pattern nearly always fails before the 'blow' of the shot

112

I say 'on average' very deliberately. Clearly, a gun firing dust shot would theoretically maintain its pattern beyond the point where the shot would kill. In such a case, penetration fails before pattern. But I repeat that *on average* it is the other way round.

Can we not get pattern and penetration (killing power) to fail together, and so get the best of both worlds? We can. There are two ways of doing it:

(a) Keep the shot closer together; or
(b) Use smaller shot, and so *get more pellets.*

I am assuming for the moment a constant velocity, with a constant load.

We all know that keeping the shot closer together can be done by choking the gun, and this is indeed done. By a judicious selection of choke, the pattern can often – though by no means always – be held sufficiently tight that killing power and pattern *will* fail at about the same range. We can now select our size of shot, and work it out.

I must at this stage take some figures, which I will ask you to accept as virtually proven. They can be checked by reference to various textbooks, notably those written by Burrard and Gough Thomas. They are shown as Tables 1–4 inclusive in Appendix 1.

First, let us assume that an average game bird – from pheasant to partridge or pigeon – must, in order to be killed, be hit by three pellets, each still carrying an energy of 0.86ft lb. To achieve this requires a pattern containing between 120 and 130 pellets in a 30in circle (see Table 1, Appendix 1).

Now first let us see at what range various sizes of shot still have 0.86ft lb left. If you look at Table 3 in Appendix 1 you will see that Nos 4 and 5 shot have plenty of energy at over 60yd, No 6 shot fails at 55yd and No 7 shot at 45yd. So much for the penetration side of the problem.

Now let us see how difficult it is to get 120 to 130 pellets into a 30in circle, at the fail penetration range. Let us assume $1\frac{1}{16}$oz shot as standard. Then, knowing the number of shot in the cartridge,

113

we can calculate easily the percentage of the pattern to meet the 130 requirement in the 30in circle. For instance, in $1\frac{1}{16}$oz of No 7 shot there are 361 pellets. The percentage of the pattern to meet our requirements is thus $\frac{130}{361} \times \frac{100}{1}$ or 36 per cent. It will be a higher percentage for larger shot. No 4 shot, with half the pellets, will require 72 per cent of the pattern in the 30in circle.

Now let us see what barrel borings will give this and other percentages for different-sized shot at fail penetration range.

Shot size	Percentage pattern in 30in circle required to kill	Range where 'blow' fails	Boring which will give percentage pattern at range
7	36%	45yd	True cylinder
6	45%	55yd	Full choke
5	56%	Over 60yd	Not possible
4	72%	Over 60yd	Not possible

See also Table 2, Appendix 1.

This table shows that:

(a) Big shot means fewer pellets, and so it becomes more difficult to maintain pattern.
(b) No 7 shot is sufficient against all medium game birds (including pigeon!) up to 45yd.
(c) We can at the same time afford to use an open-bored gun, which will obviously make it easier for us to shoot well.
(d) Any bigger shot may (but may not!) give an increase in range and then only *at a price*.

Let us see what bigger shot *will* achieve, and at what cost. Suppose we insist on a killing range of 50yd.

(a) *No 7 shot*. Will not kill.
(b) *No 6 shot*. Because there are fewer pellets, we have to insist on 45 per cent of the shot charge to ensure a good enough pattern. At 50yd, this can be achieved by $\frac{3}{4}$ choke (see Table 2, Appendix 1).

But surely reducing the spread of the shot makes it harder

114

to shoot well. To reduce the spread *unnecessarily* is foolish. In actual fact, the spread of a true cylinder is roughly twice that thrown by $\frac{3}{4}$ choke (true at short ranges, and not quite so accurate at longer ranges).

We are thus clearly making it much more difficult for ourselves to shoot well – twice as difficult at short range – solely to increase our effective range from 45yd to 50yd.

(c) *No 5 shot.* Because of the yet smaller total number of pellets, we have to increase our percentage in a 30in circle to 56 per cent. Even with full choke, this can only be achieved at slightly over 45yd.

The loss of spread is even more severe with a full choke than with a $\frac{3}{4}$ charge and No 6 shot (above). In fact, now the spread is less than half that of a true cylinder, and we have gained virtually nothing in effective range. *We have made it twice as hard for ourselves, for minimal gain.*

(d) *No 4 shot.* Still fewer pellets in the total charge. Therefore we have to raise the percentage of the total charge in a 30in circle to 72 per cent. With a full choke, this is just about possible at 40yd. Thus we have to depend upon a really tight pattern which makes it yet *harder* for us to shoot well, *and* achieves a *reduction* in effective range.

These results are so illuminating that it is worth seeing what happens with other game, both larger and smaller.

Duck and hare

We will assume that to kill hare and duck requires three pellets each of 1.0ft lb, and requires 100 pellets in a 30in circle to ensure that the pattern is sufficiently dense. Then the following table gives the true picture.

Shot size	Percentage pattern	Range where 'blow' fails	Boring
7	28%	40–50yd*	True cylinder
6	35%	50yd	Imp cylinder
5	43%	55yd	Full choke
4	55%	Over 60yd	Not possible

* 'Blow' fails at 40yd. Pattern good up to 50.

From this we can deduce the following facts for heavy game:

(a) *No 7 shot*. Good and advantageous out to 40yd. You are getting the maximum chance of hitting because of the large spread of a true cylinder.

(b) *No 6 shot*. Using an improved cylinder this is almost ideal. Effective to 50yd.

(c) *No 5 shot*. If you can accept 50yd as a maximum range, you can get away with $\frac{1}{2}$ choke or perhaps $\frac{3}{4}$ choke. This is definitely of less value than No 6 shot, because we have the *same* effective range, and a *tighter* spread.

(d) *No 4 shot*. To achieve our 55 per cent pattern, we require a $\frac{3}{4}$ choke which will be effective only to 45yd (full choke will not manage a good enough pattern at 50yd). We thus *lose* 5yd in range with no compensating advantage.

Snipe

Let us now examine the smaller bird such as a snipe. To kill such a bird we require a blow of 0.5ft lb per pellet. Two pellets are sufficient, and the minimum pattern required is 270.

The table is then as follows:

Shot size	Percentage pattern	Range where 'blow' fails	Boring
7	$77\frac{1}{2}\%$	60yd	Not possible even with full choke
6	100%	Over 60yd	Not possible even with full choke
5	100%	Over 60yd	Not possible even with full choke
4	100%	Over 60yd	Not possible even with full choke

You can thus see that, even with No 7 shot, we have not got enough pellets, but have too much energy. We *must* therefore use No 8 or even No 9 shot against snipe.

Conclusions

Our conclusions are inescapable. Basically we are going to get the best results by reducing the size of the shot and thus getting *more pellets*; and opening the bore of the gun and thus, incidentally, making it easier for ourselves to shoot well.

We can prove this because we can see that for normal game shooting:

(a) No 7 shot and a true cylinder is best for 'medium' game.
(b) No 6 shot and improved cylinder is best for duck and hare.
(c) No 7 shot is actually *too big* for snipe.
(d) *Any* form of choke (other than improved cylinder) is no advantage whatever. It is a disadvantage.
(e) Any shot larger than No 6 is disadvantageous.

To tighten the pattern and use heavier shot will almost certainly make it more difficult for ourselves, or actually reduce the effective range. *Or both!*

And isn't this borne out in practice? Some mathematicians can prove a theory and then, opening their eyes from their intense concentration, look round to see if they are right. The more humble of us do it the other way round.

Practical experience came first in my case. I was doing a lot of snipe shooting in Ceylon, and used No 8 shot, which was very effective. As I was without knowledge in those days, I always took a number of cartridges loaded with No 4 shot for the odd duck that we might meet. Now as everyone knows, this does not work! Never is there time to load with No 4 if duck are coming. If No 4 is loaded, there is not time to take it out again when a snipe gets up.

It was quickly apparent that my snipe shooting was a great deal poorer with No 4 shot. When I connected, the bird was almost always wounded, having of course been hit by one pellet only. And the duck seemed to collapse very satisfactorily when I held straight with No 8 shot.

The conclusion is the exact opposite of what most people believe, namely that small shot and an open bore have the greatest scope for wounding. I repeat that this is untrue. It is the shot big in proportion to the size of the bird that will wound most often. This is what the expert says, though he often puts it in a slightly different way.

It was this *practical* demonstration that started me off. Of course you may say that a few shots like this prove nothing: in answer I can only say that I realised at the time that I would never have snipe shooting of this calibre again, and so I went flat out for it. To give you an idea, two of us once got 101 snipe in the day.

You may say that No 4 shot with snipe is an extreme example. But would not many of us, if we really wanted to shoot a snipe a very long way out, put in a cartridge loaded with No 5 (or even No 4), saying, 'If you put the centre of the pattern from a full choke on him even at 50yd or more, down he'll come?' I can assure you that he would *not*!

Thus I came to the conclusion that we normally use shot that is too big. If we say that shot is 'too big', what do we mean? Surely that the 'blow' is too great, and thus that a smaller shot will have enough.

As soon as we say this, we can perhaps begin to think of the boring of the gun, for the 'blow' of a certain sized shot will be the same whether it is fired from a full cylinder or a full choke. Being quick in the uptake, the deduction took me about ten years, and then (of course) was arrived at practically, and not, I regret to say, by any simple mental thought or calculation.

Often I come up against the young man who is a complete beginner. He has bought a cheapish foreign gun, almost invariably with a lot of choke in both barrels. As soon as he hits a clay, and I see only a cloud of dust at about 25yd, I give an inward groan. I know from bitter experience that however well he shoots, he is going to miss three out of ten, because he is shooting with too tight a pattern. I can see the shot on these occasions miss the clay by a very small margin. When I am with such a pupil, I can encourage and explain. But when he is by himself, these inevitable misses may well come together and confidence will disappear.

You will say, of course, that you must have a tight pattern for a small object like a clay. For an *end-on* clay a long way off I agree. So the down-the-line experts use small shot, and thus lots of it, *and* a degree of choke. But for a clay other than end-on, no choke is necessary, if cartridges with a large number of shot are used. Such a target off the 40yd-high tower can be smashed with certainty – provided you hold straight – again and again with a full-cylinder gun. If it works for a clay, it will work for a partridge or indeed something a bit bigger.

Practical experience has shown me that a full cylinder and No 7 shot are best for game. I am ramming home what I have previously tried to prove theoretically. But if I had written my ideas the other way round, I would still be up against the disbeliever, who instinctively feels that I am wrong. When confronted, he has to invent a reason for his disbelief, and often it is not a very good one.

Why No 6 shot?
Why have our great British gunmakers for so long been making gun barrels with some degree of choke and regulating them for No 6 shot, if full cylinder and No 7 shot are best?

This strikes me as the strongest argument so far used by anyone to counter my open-bore and small-shot contention. It is thus worth answering, though of course I do so without any reference to the gun trade, and am simply voicing my own ideas.

Gunmakers are in business to sell guns, and to do so they must pander to a certain degree to public opinion. If you do not believe this, think back to the tremendous row about 25in barrels which arose when Churchill first introduced them on his guns. Barrels of this length are now quite accepted, in fact are more in fashion than the normal length of 30in common at the time. But Churchill had to be a brave man, and without the courage of absolute conviction might well have failed and gone out of business.

Now No 7 shot has its limitations. It will not kill average game as far as 50yd with certainty, whether it be fired from a full

119

cylinder or full choke. People demanded – and still do – a gun that will kill up to this range. The fact that such a demand approached the unreasonable was naturally not voiced as even injudicious by the gunmakers, who were quite able to satisfy the 50yd requirement – at a price, of course.

Suppose that you were a gunmaker, and a customer asked you for a gun that would consistently kill at 50yd; you would not tell him that he would rarely have occasion to fire at this range, and further, that if he did, he would not have the skill to hit his target. At least, I wouldn't! I would shrug my shoulders, and bore and regulate my gun to give sufficient pattern to kill at this range – and I would have to use No 6 shot to do it. After a bit, No 6 shot would become accepted as the smallest size that can reasonably be used against game.

I am sure that this was – and indeed is – the basic thinking. I can recall advertisements from many gunmakers, invariably quoting letters from satisfied customers who wrote, 'I fired at a sitting duck with your wonderful gun, and killed it stone dead. I paced the distance and it was 83yd.' And so on and on.

And all this was compounded by the use of choke. Clever advertising insisted that this would 'increase the range of your gun'. What is wrong with that? What has *not* been said, of course, is by how much the range would be increased, and at what cost – facts which are seldom mentioned even today.

People think that it is sheer common sense that big shot kept concentrated must kill further; and since everyone subconsciously wants a reserve of power, so to speak, up his sleeve, this is what he instinctively plumps for. The fact that this actually *reduces* the killing range of his gun as far as game is concerned, when he thinks it has increased it, is surely ironic. That he then refuses to believe that this reduction has occurred, even when told, makes some of us almost weep with frustration.

So we want a 'reserve of power' – just in case. If we insist, then we must have No 6 shot, although, as I have repeatedly said, the reserve is marginal, is never used, and makes all normal shooting much more difficult. Even then, to many of us, it is 'obvious' that if No 6 is better than No 7, then No 5 will be better than No 6. And if we want really long-range stuff, then No 4 is better still – sheer common sense surely. Although quite erroneous, the argument has a certain superficial logic, and is therefore difficult to argue against – especially if there appears to be little need to do so.

But eventually someone uses No 7 shot – probably quite by chance – and shoots rather better. That is one faltering step towards a sensible answer to the problem. And perhaps by the laws of chance alone, someone else then realises that he has got so many No 7 shot in a standard cartridge that he can get enough pattern at the maximum range of that shot without any choke at all. All he has lost is perhaps 3yd in extreme range – probably less.

Many people still do not realise this. Indeed you have only to read correspondence in the technical magazines to see that. And so they continue to use No 6 shot, and then they must use some choke, or their pattern will fail quite early. The gunmaker is delighted to bow to your demand, and regulate your gun to fire this No 6 shot, and may spend hours on the choking to ensure that the comparatively narrow pattern is regularly filled.

And guess who pays for the highly skilled labour so long employed on this useless task.

How to choose your first gun

This is a most difficult section to write. It would be very much easier if I could see you and talk to you. At least I would then know how big physically you were, how old, and what you expected to shoot; and lastly I might be able to find out how rich (or poor) you were.

There are, in short, four factors which will influence your choice of gun. These are:

(a) How much you can afford.
(b) How big you are physically, or perhaps how old.

(c) What you hope to shoot.

(d) How keen you are.

Perhaps the most important factor is how keen you are. I am going to assume that you have done a little shooting and that the bug has bitten you. If you are doubtful of whether you are going to enjoy yourself, do not spend too much on any gun. I repeat that I am assuming you are keen, and it is on this basis that I shall try to help.

If you are between eighteen and sixty years old, you will probably be physically big and strong enough to handle most guns. It is outside these limits that physical disability may become a serious factor.

The young boy

For the young boy, the .410 must be a gun to be considered. It can be handled by the average-sized boy of eleven, but usually not before. But it has a small spread and a small 'blow', and it is perhaps a bit unfair to start a small boy off with something that requires a good deal of accuracy. If the boy is keen enough, it is well worth it; if he is only lukewarm, *wait*. Borrow one if necessary to see how keen he is. You will get your reward.

All guns, including the .410, are expensive. Are there any boys growing out of theirs from whom you can buy? And are there any younger brothers or friends to whom the gun can later be passed on?

You can save money by getting a single barrel, but consider carefully before buying a bolt-action model or a hammer gun at this stage. Some of the bolt-action models – those worked like rifles – are pigs to load and to handle. Hammer guns – those whose hammers are located above the lock, and have to be cocked before they can be released by pulling the trigger – are not for weak fingers and thumbs: they are too dangerous.

Under-eighteens and over-sixties

There are those who may find difficulty in handling the weight of the average gun. For these people, only the 20-bore, the 16-bore and the 12-bore 'light' guns need to be considered. There are guns in other bores, but they have no material advantages over 20, 16 or 12, in fact several disadvantages.

The 20-bore weighs between $5\frac{1}{4}$ and $5\frac{3}{4}$ lb; the 16, $5\frac{1}{2}$ –6lb; and the 'light' 12-bore, $5\frac{3}{4}$ –$6\frac{1}{4}$lb. Virtually the only limitation which lack of years, or excess of them, imposes is on the weight of the gun that can easily be carried. The lack of weight in the gun imposes also one limitation on the firer, and that is the quantity of shot (i.e. the shot load) that can be fired at a time. It might just be possible, in exceptional circumstances, to get a 20-bore to fire a full 12-bore load of shot, if you chambered the gun suitably and got a special cartridge.

A 12-bore gun weighing say 7lb could absorb the opposite and equal reaction of pushing out over an ounce of shot at a normal velocity without bruising your shoulder. A 20-bore weighing say 5lb would not. The effect on the shooter in such a case would be disastrous. The lighter gun – whatever its bore – is thus limited as to the charge of shot that it can fire, purely by the inability of the firer to absorb the recoil.

It is not always known that the spread (from similar choked barrels and at similar ranges) of a 20-bore, a 16-bore and a 12-bore is the same. If there are fewer shot in a 20-bore cartridge, as there must be, our *pattern* is going to fail earlier. (This applies to a lesser degree to the 16, and less still to a 'light' 12-bore.) In other words, the effective range of these guns is less than that of the 'standard' 12-bore.

It will not be reduced very much. In fact if you use No 7 shot and full cylinder, you have a 20-bore effective against medium game (pigeons, partridges, pheasants etc) up to 37yd, and better than that of course for the 16-bore and better still for the 'light' 12-bore.

This seems a very small price to pay for being able to handle your gun easily. The lighter the gun, the more range you will have to lose.

You can of course make up this loss of range a bit by choking your gun. You will get a bit of range back, and you will lose a lot of spread which will make your shooting more difficult. I know which way round I would like to have it.

Now for the *type of gun* for the under-eighteens and over-sixties. Since you are limited in weight, the gun must be either a single-barrel or a side-by-side double. You will not wish to pay a lot of money for the boy, even if there are a lot of younger brothers coming on, so a single barrel is a possibility here. But single-barrel guns are often comparatively clumsy weapons. If you can afford it, I would suggest a double-barrel hammerless gun.

Let me say straight away that for the over-sixty you should get the best gun you can afford. (This applies to other people, but at the moment we are considering those people who can only handle a light gun.) A best London gun will cost the earth – and is worth it. Any object which has been fashioned for long hours by skilled hands is always a beautiful thing, and a best London gun is a very good example of this. It will cost you the same whether it is a 12-bore, a 'light' 12, a 16 or a 20-bore (or even a .410, for that matter). It will last you, your son, and his son, and longer, if reasonably looked after. It will handle and function beautifully. It will appreciate in value. Having whetted your appetite, I will not spoil it by telling you the cost.

So far, we have narrowed the choice to a double-barrelled gun of a weight that can be conveniently carried and handled. For the people we are considering at the moment, this must hold good irrespective of what they intend to shoot. Our choice is thus easier: now that we have decided on the weight and type of gun, the choice will depend solely on cost. As always, you have to pay for what you get. So let us see what we can do without, if we must.

Side lock or box lock? Box lock is cheaper and a bit lighter. It is perhaps marginally inferior in a number of ways to a side lock, but on balance, for what we are considering, it will save money to go for a box lock.

Single trigger or double trigger? The single trigger is complicated, expensive and basically less reliable. There is, for a beginner, not much advantage – therefore double trigger.

Ejector or non-ejector? All guns have what is known as primary ejection: that is, the cartridge, whether fired or not, is lifted clear of the breech when the gun is opened, so that it can be easily lifted out with the fingers. An ejector gun ejects the fired cartridge (and only the fired one) clear of the gun when the gun is opened. It is thus quicker and more easy to reload.

Do you really want an ejector? They add greatly to the cost, and to the complication. The complication in the cheaper gun may cause a loss of reliability.

Engraving. Avoid engraving, which is expensive, and which will not help you to kill a bird in any way.

New or second-hand? A good English second-hand gun may well prove a bargain. It may be possible to pick up a pedigree non-ejector, for example, at a very reasonable price. But there are snags in the second-hand market of guns, in the same way as there are snags in the second-hand motor-car market.

Remember we are at this stage considering 'light' 12-bores, 16-bores, 20-bores or .410s only. The number of these on the second-hand market is limited.

Your source therefore is either:

(a) the *reputable* dealer, from whom the good second-hand gun can never be cheap.

(b) Friends who have boys or 'family' light guns available, and on whom you can rely.

(c) Advertised sources. This means ideally seeking the help of a really knowledgeable friend.

In short, you just may be able to get a really good gun well suited to you at a reasonable price on the second-hand market. But as a beginner, you are more likely to get something less than ideal for *you*.

New guns. There are several makers, both English and foreign, who make good guns well below the top price. Many of them make 16- and 20-bore guns, which will come within your 'weight of gun' category. You can probably rule out the 'light' 12, which has to be carefully designed to achieve a light weight and is therefore expensive.

You will be buying a comparatively mass-produced article – indeed like the average car – which will take a bit of running in, and conceivably may develop initially a minor fault or two, though these can easily be put right.

It is possible to buy a foreign gun 'in the white' – that is, in its basic condition, made with very good materials – and then subsequently have it 'tuned up' to your requirements. By tuning up, I mean having it passed for British Proof, stock fitted to your measurements, barrels blued and so on. To give you an idea of the costs involved, the price of the gun itself in the white might be about £200. To have the gun fully 'tuned up', engraved and so on would cost a further £250.

You can buy a foreign double-barrelled gun for less than this, but the above paragraph will give you an idea of how little can be devoted to the 'tuning up' of any gun if it is not to cost a good deal.

Summary. For the under-eighteen and the over-sixty, get a double-barrelled side-by-side gun with two triggers, of a bore, and thus a weight, to suit the user. To save money, go for a box lock and a non-ejector – no engraving. It should, I think, be new, but it can be of a foreign imported make. Within the limitations I have suggested, pay as much as you can. You will not be disappointed. There is one proviso for the over-sixty. Pick up, handle and if possible shoot a best gun to see what it is like. If you can afford it, buy it. You have after all only about thirty years left to enjoy it, and this is only just long enough to get the full pleasure that such a lovely thing can give you.

What will you have if you buy a new gun of the type I have recommended, probably for under £200, and maybe for less than half this sum?

The disadvantages are that the gun will be:

(a) Rather stiff to open and close and operate initially.
(b) Comparatively clumsy compared with what can be achieved by expensive weapons.
(c) Almost certainly too heavily choked in both barrels.
(d) Not fitted to your measurements as regards stock, which is not too important.

On the other hand, you will have a gun which:

(a) Will be to your weight.
(b) Will be a good killer.
(c) Will prove basically reliable.
(d) Within its known limitations, will do what you want and will give you pleasure.

Choice for the average man

So far we have considered only those people whose choice of weapon is limited by the weight they can reasonably carry around. For the average man, this consideration is not nearly so important, and thus a wider choice becomes available.

A new factor can now be catered for in the choice of weapon. *What are you going to shoot?*
This can be divided into four categories:

(a) Wildfowl shooting.
(b) Game and rough shooting.
(c) Down-the-line clay pigeon shooting.
(d) Skeet shooting.

And ideally, a different gun will be best for each category. Do not be alarmed. One gun will, in practice, be pretty well all right for all these categories. But if you are going to concentrate on one type of shooting, then one particular type of gun will suit you better.

Wildfowl. Most duck are heavy birds that require a heavy shot blow. Duck are also very wary and so one tends to have to shoot at long ranges. Both these factors often require you to have a gun heavy enough to throw a heavy load of shot. It may thus be desirable to have a 12-bore gun chambered for 3in cartridges which will contain a large number of pellets.

But do *not* get a gun which is too heavily choked or too heavy. Both these factors may make it too difficult for you to shoot well; and remember, you will sometimes want to use your gun against rabbits, pigeon and perhaps game.

I would suggest a double-barrelled 12-bore, $2\frac{3}{4}$in chambers, improved cylinder and $\frac{1}{2}$ choke, two triggers and perhaps ejector; as good as you can afford. Weight not more than $7\frac{1}{4}$lb, preferably less; if you insist, a similar weapon, but with 3in chambers and inevitably a bit heavier. If you buy this latter weapon, and accept more choke (as everyone will advise you), you will no doubt *think* that you will kill more duck, but you will in fact bag fewer.

I have not recommended an over-and-under, nor a 'pump' gun. I believe the place for both these guns is in the clay pigeon field, and they are discussed later.

Game and rough shooting. What I have written about the under-eighteens and over-sixties applies here. The gun I would recommend would be a 12-bore hammerless ejector with two triggers and 'straight' grip. Weight about $6\frac{1}{2}$lb, $2\frac{1}{2}$in chambers, and bored full cylinder and improved cylinder. As expensive as you can afford.

Let me take the last point first. The more you pay, the more you will get. If you pay a lot for your gun, you will have a weapon that will be a joy to look at, and certainly a great pleasure to handle (of which I shall say more in a moment). It will function perfectly: the trigger pulls will be crisp and of the correct weight, the ejection will be identical for each barrel and strong, the gun will be easy to open whether fired or not, and to close, and every piece of the mechanism will work like silk. It will throw a pattern for which it has been designed every time, and it will last.

Finally, it will have a natural 'pointability'. This is difficult to describe, but very easy to appreciate when you have such a gun in your hands. Some makers seem to have the knack of achieving this – and some have not. The fact remains that a best gunmaker can achieve a gun that 'feels' wonderful. You will, in short, shoot better in spite of yourself.

I believe that part of the answer to this question of 'pointability' lies in the designer incorporating most of the weight of the gun in its centre so that it is concentrated more between the hands when you are mounting.

Suppose, for the sake of argument, that a 12-bore gun weighing $6\frac{1}{2}$lb could be made with fibreglass barrels and fibreglass butt, both of feather weight. Then it is obvious that you would be handling a weapon with virtually all the weight between your hands, and it would be almost as easy to point as your own finger. Skilled gunmakers today are near to achieving this, but unfortunately I do not believe it is the absolute ideal for which we should aim. A highly 'pointable' gun is all right so far as it goes, but it may lack stability and momentum.

By stability I am talking about the ability of the gun to keep steadily on the target: and if it gets *on* quickly, it may tend to get *off* quickly. By momentum, I mean the ability of the gun to help the swing to keep going. There is certainly one maker of the highest class whose guns seem to me to be 'nose heavy'; I am sure this was designed in deliberately, but I personally find these guns a bit sulky to point.

Another factor to be considered is the length of the barrel. Men who shoot are conservative people, and it takes a long time to change ideas – or perhaps prejudices. Up to the end of the nineteenth century, black powder (gunpowder) was used as a propellant in cartridges. Gunpowder had many assets as a propellant, probably the greatest being that it gave the charge of shot a comparatively slow push out of the barrel. You can *hear* this, if you go to a game fair and watch the 'old-fashioned' shooters firing at clays with black powder and muzzle-loaders.

This slow push required a comparatively long barrel – 32in

129

was probably ideal – to enable the slow-burning propellant to develop sufficient muzzle velocity. When the modern quick-burning propellants came in, it took about forty years for people to realise that a long barrel was no longer necessary.

It was Churchill who introduced the 25in barrel. There was at the time a most long-drawn and fierce fight between the XXV School and the 30in barrel advocates. Now that the dust of this controversy has subsided a bit, we can perhaps look at it all in a more objective way.

First, we can take it as fact that the reduction in muzzle velocity developed by a 25in barrel, compared with say a 30in barrel, is negligible. It is there, admittedly, but is so small that it can be ignored. It may also be accepted that there is no deterioration in pattern produced as a result of the different length of barrel. Finally, with a raised rib, both barrels *seem* the same length when you are shooting.

What then are the advantages and disadvantages of the short barrel over the longer, 'normal' barrel?

(a) The shorter barrel enables more weight to be concentrated in the centre of the gun, and therefore it becomes more 'pointable'.

(b) The gun can be made lighter.

(c) It is at present fashionable!

The disadvantage is that for a big man with long arms the stock becomes long and the gun with short barrels then looks out of proportion. This is not quite such a silly argument as it may seem. Whatever it is, a thing must *look* right to be right. The ease of pointability of a gun probably matters less to a big strong man, and so he can take advantage of the increased momentum and increased stability of the longer barrel.

To sum up, I believe that the short-barrelled gun has advantages for most of us. On the other hand, when I am lucky enough to shoot with two guns, I cannot tell in a hot corner whether I have got my 25in-barrelled gun or the 28in in my hand.

Down-the-line clay pigeon shooting. The two basic types of clay shooting, down-the-line and skeet or sporting shooting, demand different guns. I will concentrate first on the requirements for down-the-line shooting.

The most usual type of gun used by the best shots at this sport is the over-and-under. The reason is the ease of getting on to the clay given by a 'single' barrel. And this is overwhelming.

There are indeed some disadvantages in an over-and-under. These may be summarised as follows:

(a) It is heavy.
(b) It is comparatively clumsy.
(c) The gun has to be opened through a big angle to enable the lower barrel to be loaded.

These disadvantages are apparent in game and rough shooting, but do not matter at all in down-the-line shooting; in fact, the heaviness may be a positive help on occasion.

Since you are firing at an end-on clay target at longish ranges, pattern is everything. To this end, since a very small 'blow' will break a clay, plenty of small shot is used – the heavy gun helps to reduce the recoil felt by the shooter – and both barrels are heavily choked. (Since you are always firing at long ranges, the disadvantage of a small spread at short ranges can be accepted.) In addition, the rib on the top of the barrel is raised and ventilated, so that when the gun gets hot the cool rib will not heat the air above it and so 'bend' the line of sight between gun and clay. Handling and pointability do not particularly matter, since the gun is mounted to the shoulder before the clay is called.

I believe the over-and-under *could* be a very successful game gun. At least two makers have produced an elegant and not too heavy over-and-under, although they are expensive. I wonder if the disadvantage of having to have a wide-opening gun could not be overcome by allowing the gun to open sideways.

There is also the automatic gun, which has a big advantage for down-the-line shooting because of its single barrel. Again it is heavy and comparatively clumsy and difficult to load quickly. But it is often possible to get varying degrees of choke in the form of an adaptor. These adaptors can be screwed on to the end of the barrel, and thus the gun becomes more flexible to use than the true over-and-under down-the-line gun.

It certainly can be used for rough shooting and wildfowl, but is not suitable for shooting game in large numbers.

Skeet or sporting shooting. Skeet shooting in particular is done at short ranges. All that has been written about game guns applies here except that, since there is virtually no need to fire at over 30yd, the gun to use ideally requires full-cylinder boring, and short barrels to achieve quick pointing.

In fact I should not be surprised if, one day, guns specifically to be used for skeet shooting were bored slightly 'bell-mouthed', on the lines of the old blunderbuss, solely to increase the spread.

Buying the gun

When I have the nerve to criticise a particularly outrageous hat that my wife has bought, she says, 'But dear, it's *me*.' Although I cannot always go along with this, I can understand the 'logic' behind it. It may well be the truth so far as you and a gun are concerned.

It is so easy for me to give advice, and often difficult or impossible for you to put this into practice. But if you are going to spend money on a comparatively small article, it is perhaps worth while having a counsel of perfection to work to.

Talk to your friends. Get as much advice as you can; gradually your need will clarify, so that you will get a picture of what you want. Go to your local gunmaker and talk to him; handle as many guns as you can. Do not be influenced by fancy engraving. Finally, put a limit on the price you are prepared to pay.

Can you ask to attend your local clay pigeon club? They will always welcome someone who will work the traps. It will not be long before the members are showing you their guns and you will be able to feel and compare for yourself.

A small boy has a strong tendency to lean back to counter the weight of the gun when he mounts it

I repeat, this is a counsel of perfection. Whatever you buy, you will, within reason, get value for money. And perhaps what you have read in this chapter may help you to get a gun that is *you*!

When to start a boy shooting

This depends almost entirely on two factors, namely keenness and physical strength and size.

A young boy who is not desperately keen on having a go is frankly at a disadvantage if he has to start shooting with a .410.

133

It is relatively difficult to hit a moving target with the small spread given by such a small gun, and success is all-important at this early stage. It might perhaps be better to keep an interest simmering until he is physically big enough to handle a 20-bore. In short, a young boy has got to be keen, and, probably just as important, has to be given great encouragement at once.

The other factor is physical size and strength. A boy of eleven can usually handle a .410. But a small boy has a strong tendency to lean back to counter the comparatively large weight of the gun when he mounts it, which of course is wrong.

Whatever you do, do not give him too big a gun too soon. This is really dictated solely by the physical size of the boy. Give him a 20-bore too early, and the recoil may give him a knock and frighten him. It may cause him to flinch, a habit which, if acquired at this stage, will last for a very long time. Do not risk it. Keep him on a little gun and encourage and encourage and encourage.

A small boy is often extremely keen. Under these conditions, I believe all should be subordinated to getting him to hit the clays. This gives encouragement. He must of course be given opportunity to *fire* his gun. If you want a small boy, keen on shooting, to burst emotionally, give him a gun and tell him he cannot fire it. But again, he must only fire it under expert tuition. So get him firing it at moving targets with someone teaching who knows what he is about.

Do everything you can to encourage. If he is big enough, put him on a bigger gun – always with the proviso that it must *under no circumstances* be too big from the mounting and recoil angle. I am advocating a bigger gun only so that the target becomes easier to hit and he is thus given encouragement. There are major snags in giving a young boy a gun too big for him, and these far outweigh any advantages.

Of course, if you get a boy so keen that he can overcome the inevitable disappointments, and if you encourage him enough, the rewards are enormous. First, he will never be a bad shot. (This would be a turn-up for most of us!) This is because he will find it comparatively difficult to learn bad habits, because the right habits will have been ingrained. He will never revert to bad shooting habits in moments of stress – as the rest of us do – because he will never have had bad shooting habits. When things go wrong, a small correction will put them right – no need to take the whole swing to pieces and put it together again.

He will have a firm foundation for ever, on which to build his skill.

Best guns

Anything fashioned for long hours by skilled hands automatically becomes a beautiful thing. I believe it is impossible to find an example to prove this contention false. Workmanship is everything, and I do not suppose the skill available from man's hands has improved over the last three or four thousand years: think of Tutankhamun's gold mask – surely perfection! This workmanship can be recognised instantly by even the most insensitive. Of course, in mechanical things, design has improved, but good workmanship, when it is unstintingly applied, has remained constant.

Sporting guns are a typical example. I believe that virtually anyone could pick up a best gun, handle it briefly, and tell it from a mass-produced gun. This is probably obvious, but I believe it would still be true if a hand-made gun were to be compared with a machine-made gun, even if the latter were manufactured to the finest tolerances and the engraving produced by a computer. I will go further still and say that I *know* this to be a fact. The inspector of one of the best London gunmakers told me personally that when a 'finished' gun was placed before him for passing, he could tell at once when handling it which workmen had been responsible for the fitting of various parts. And I have no reason to disbelieve him.

A best gun must take at least several hundred hours to build. If this time is spent on building and fitting together an article with comparatively few working parts, surely such an article becomes

135

a work of art in its own right. Just as much work by skilled hands has gone into its making as would be bestowed on a fine picture, a beautiful clock or an ornament.

(In parentheses, we may remark that a gun is then taken outside in all weathers, and expected to withstand the shock of an explosion pretty frequently. You would not do that to your Knibb grandfather clock, which, for all the skill put into its making, has – to say the least – a quieter life!)

The snag about achieving perfection is, of course, the time required. If we want something quickly, we do not get the best – ever. If we can wait, it is then *possible* to get the best, but of course it is expensive. The more hurried this world becomes, the more expensive is time-consuming skill. Rather under a hundred years ago, a best gun cost £65. Today it would be over £5,000.

You may say that it is fantastic to pay this much for a gun. But they said just the same in 1886 when they had to pay their £65. You have only to read the books on shooting from the Badminton Library series, published in the late nineteenth century, to see proof after proof that the 'high' sum was money well spent. The same is true today.

What do you get for your money? First, you obtain a great deal of inbuilt skill. This alone is priceless – it shows at once. It is almost a curious feeling to handle a best gun, for it seems to have a feeling of life about it.

Of course it works most beautifully. It opens and closes like silk, and everything seems effortless and smooth. And it will continue to be like this – with reasonable maintenance – for a great many years. It shoots where you point it, with regularity of pattern always, and consistently. Finally, for those who have eyes to see, it looks beautiful.

All these, you may say, are niceties, for which you might be willing to pay a bit over the odds – but surely not twenty times the price of a good, sound, workmanlike gun which in its turn would give years of pleasure. There are, I suppose, some people

(*opposite*) Good workmanship, unstintingly applied, has remained constant

who could not understand these 'niceties' even if they could afford the money. But a great many people can and indeed do appreciate all the inbuilt beauty of appearance, handling and performance of a best gun. This combination of perfection always has and always will cost a lot of money: that many shrewd people have always thought the cost worthwhile is surely a pointer.

How a best gun is built
It is a revelation to visit the workshops of Holland & Holland, Gunmakers Ltd. In an age of mass-production, the care and patience of skilled men is something to wonder at. In short, the finished article made in these workshops must rank as a major achievement in man's long search for perfection.

And it is perfection that Holland & Holland are seeking with every best gun that they produce. Twenty-five per cent of the work is done by machines; the rest is hand-made and fitted. This proportion is governed by common sense. Where $\frac{1}{4}$in of metal has to be removed, it is done, quickly, by a machine; where a 'thou' has to be taken off, it is done, more accurately, by hand.

Every part of a best gun is made on the premises except for the rough barrel forgings, the locks, and the French walnut blanks for the stocks. All machined bits, metal or wood, come from the machine shop – the barrels, roughly bored and shaped, the actions, locks, triggers, ejectors and so on – all in the rough. Simplifying slightly, it is more or less true to say that all 'bits' designed to fit into others come from the machine shop oversize, whereas any bit designed to receive another part is machined out undersize.

It is the job of the action shop to fit the bits together. This is all done by hand, using the smoke method to ensure the perfect fit of every part. As an example, the barrels have to be so fitted to the action that when the gun is closed there is a perfect fit between them. The barrel ends and lumps are held over a candle so that the metal which is to make contact with the action is slightly darkened by the smoke of the candle. The barrels are fitted to the action and then taken off again. The smoke-darkened parts will show light shiny patches where they have made contact with the action, and these patches are removed with a very fine file. The whole process is then repeated until all the metal is evenly bright after the gun has been closed and opened. The tolerance is *nil*: the fit is accurate to the size of a particle of smoke.

All parts are fitted to each other like this, including the locks let in to the wooden stock. All this takes time, patience and great skill. For instance, it takes an average of seventeen hours to ensure the perfect fit and working of the safety catch; to fit the extractors to the barrels, slightly longer.

The barrels, before reaching the action shop, are brazed together and bored full choke in the barrel shop. Extreme care is taken to ensure that the two barrels are level and parallel.

One more example of the quest for perfection: when the barrels have been fitted to the action, great trouble is taken to ensure that the hole bored in the action to take the striker is dead central with regard to the barrels. Thus, if the cartridge is round and the percussion cap central (as it always is), the striker will hit the cap bang in the middle every time. If you do not own a best gun, have a look at one of your fired cartridges. Has the percussion cap been struck dead central? Or nearly? Or even to one side?

When the gun is roughly fitted together, it is all checked. This takes one man eleven hours. Anything not perfect is corrected.

The stock is fitted to the gun in the stocking shop. The customer will usually choose his stock of French walnut in the rough. It will take fifty-five hours to fit the stock to the gun and let in the locks. It will take a further seventeen to shape the stock to the customer's measurements, and yet a further fifteen hours to 'polish' it. The 'polishing' is done by hand with linseed oil and a very fine abrasive, rather as a pair of shoes or boots used to be 'boned'. (I personally can remember a soldier being reprimanded for apparently going on parade in patent-leather boots. They shone like glass; he knew how to bone good leather.)

The gun is next sent to the shooting school, where a man

called a regulator, who must possess a high degree of a peculiar skill, alters the degree, shape, and practically every other dimension of the choke, to ensure that the gun always shoots to the percentage pattern specified by the customer.

Then the gun goes back to the engraving shop, where the work is of course all done by hand. A 'standard' Holland & Holland engraving will take about seventy hours. An engraving of a special nature might take up to four hundred hours. One of the engravers gave, as an example of such an engraving, a picture of the owner's favourite dog chasing a pheasant. It made me grin to find this small 'imperfection' amongst so much perfection.

The engravers themselves said that they never stopped learning, and that they reckoned it took forty years to produce a really good engraver. I saw their practice plates. These are flat pieces of metal measuring about 5in by 2in and originally about $\frac{1}{4}$in thick. They are engraved with various parts of standard designs, purely as practice. When the plates are completely covered, the engravings are rubbed off and the process is repeated. The plates I saw were all paper-thin. I asked how good an engraver was at the end of this: one replied that after this amount of practice he had been allowed to engrave the head of one screw in a gun.

Finally the gun is passed to the finishing shop, where it is taken to pieces and the whole action is regulated, trigger pulls are adjusted and so on. This takes about seventy hours.

Here is a firm striving for perfection. To use their own words, they try to offer quality and integrity. These are attributes that are not commonly spoken of today, so it is all the more welcome when we see a product that obviously embodies both.

It will take two years from the date of placing an order to receive your gun. The gun will not look superficially very different from any other. But as soon as you handle it and use it, it will at once be apparent that such a gun incorporates a great deal of skill laboriously acquired. When you have paid for this, it will cost a lot in pound notes, but if you can afford it, you will have bought something pretty near priceless dirt cheap.

Naturally there are other best gunmakers in London and other cities. I do not doubt that they produce weapons of a similar class, and in a similar way to the one I have briefly described. They must produce very good weapons to stay in business – and most have been in business a great number of years.

5 Behaviour When Shooting

Safety

You may kill, or you may miss
But at all times remember this
All the pheasants ever bred
Won't repay for one man dead.

When you hold a shotgun, you have a lethal weapon in your hand. At close range, not only can it kill your friend, but it can kill you. At longer ranges it will wound or blind.

I am therefore going to divide safety drill up into two factors: *handling*, which affects you and your friends close to, and *firing*, which is more likely to affect your friends further away.

Remember at the outset that, as you read this, you will not see yourself as ever being dangerous. Very few people do anything with a gun that is deliberately unsafe. Or, to put it another way, they always think they are safe. *This applies to all of us.* So if someone tells you that you may be unsafe with a gun, when you know you are perfectly all right, you may well be disbelieving. In our own eyes, it is *never* our fault. (How seldom, if ever, have you heard someone, when describing a car accident in which he has been involved, admit it was his own mistake!)

Let us make certain we never have a shooting accident. Here are some rules.

Handling

When you get a gun into your hand open it to see if it is loaded. I can always tell the man who has done a bit of shooting: I hand him his gun, and see if he opens it. If he does, all is well. If he does not, watch out! You must do it, *always*. I am constantly opening my gun to make quite sure it is empty. I remember a man who was a safe gun. He was getting into a Land Rover after a drive,

142

When not shooting – *unload*. This applies when talking with other people or when by oneself

and for the fortieth time opened his gun purely from habit. He told me later that he knew it was empty. It was loaded! He has never forgotten it. Learn from his mistake.

Frequently we read of someone injured or killed when 'cleaning his gun'. This just could not happen if we always opened the gun when we picked it up.

When not shooting – unload. This applies when talking with other people, or when by oneself. To make it clear that you are unloaded, open the gun. Then everyone can see. To put the safety catch on is *not* enough. The safety catch only locks the triggers; the gun is still fully cocked. Before the gun ever leaves your hand, unload. Do not put it down for a moment without unloading.

Before you load for the first time, look through the barrels

Before you load for the first time, look through the barrels.
There may be a bit of cleaning stuff left up the barrel; there may
be a bit of snow, frozen into a lump of ice, flipped up your barrel
from someone's heel while you were walking behind him. Look
through your barrels before shooting. If there is *any* blockage,
your gun may burst on firing.

Unload when climbing a gate or hedge. This applies
particularly if you are by yourself, when you may tend to think
that it doesn't matter.

You cannot be too safe. Your gun is only completely safe when
it is unloaded. If in doubt – unload. A counsel of perfection? You
must achieve perfection in this – nothing less.

Firing
The rule is as simple as this: *do not point your gun towards
anyone.* Of course! You never would. But it is very easy to do so,
and you must be severely on your guard. Let us take some
examples which may occur when walking up.

Unload when climbing a gate or hedge

A bird gets up behind you, and you turn round and shoot it. Did you *know* no one was behind you – perhaps stopped to pick up a bird?

The bird goes forward low and you fire. Is the hedge at the end of the field in range, and is anyone behind it? Do you *know*?

The bird swings round right and you shoot. How close to your next-door 'gun' or beater? Or the man beyond slightly out of line? Not only must you not fire, but you must not point the gun at the bird. You are breaking the rule if you do!

I, as a young boy, was brought up with the rule that if I ever pointed my gun at anyone, I was sent home. My cousin and I, both aged about fourteen, were asked by his father to shoot partridges for the first time. We had both been looking forward to this like mad for many weeks – a lifetime it seemed. It was a lovely day and the place was stiff with birds. The first covey got up: my cousin swung down the line (he did not fire) and was sent straight home. His disappointment was agony to see. Last day of the holidays, and so nothing to shoot at for three months! But he was always a safe shot thereafter.

A bird swings round right and you shoot. How close to your next-door 'gun' or beater?

Do you ever point your gun unconsciously at someone when walking up, or simply when standing still? Your gun should either be pointed at the ground or up in the air. Is it *always*? If you do not know how to carry your gun, it will inevitably point at someone. If you do not know how to carry your gun when walking up, your left-hand neighbour will be able to 'see what size shot you are using'. In other words, your barrels will be pointing at him.

Do you *know* where people are? Certainly you do not between

Your gun should be pointed either at the ground ... or up in the air

drives. Therefore, no shooting *ever* between drives, and your gun
– which may or may not be put down – will be *unloaded*.

It is the low bird and the ground game that cause the danger.
Be very careful, and be seen to be careful. Driven grouse are
probably the most 'dangerous' of birds. They fly low and fast;
there is therefore a strong tendency to swing with the bird, and

It is the low bird and the ground game that cause the danger. Be very careful

you will at once break the rule if you swing too far right or left, as you will then point your gun at the next butt. You can only shoot these birds in front or behind – and certainly not even in front, when the beaters get within range.

Learn to shoot safely when you are young, and you are likely to be a safe shot. If you learn to shoot when you are older, it is more difficult to learn to shoot safely. So if someone tells you about safety, do not take it amiss; accept it at once.

It is quite impossible to foresee every danger. If ever you are not quite sure about a safety rule, do not be afraid to ask. People are always willing to help the seeker after knowledge, and are often flattered at being questioned. It will be clear anyway that you are a beginner; by asking, you will show everyone that you are on the right track, that you appreciate the possible danger of carelessness and inexperience, and that you are doing your best to become a *safe gun*.

Conduct on the field

Grouse shooting

It is acknowledged, I think, that driven grouse are probably the most difficult birds in the world to shoot. They can also, as I have said, be the most dangerous, for the simple reason that they nearly always fly low.

The more experienced 'guns' of course know all this! Indeed there exists a generation of older men who were brought up with Edwardian severity towards safety when shooting. Such men have an enviable reputation for good manners and safe shooting. Always? Well, not quite! And it is this 'not quite' that I want to enlarge upon.

There are two factors which I have noticed in those approaching late middle age. They are factors which apply particularly to grouse driving, and I have not seen them discussed before. But they are of considerable importance for all that.

When on the moor, it is now often the habit of the head keeper to warn those in the butts by blowing a whistle when the beaters are getting in range of the guns. I do not know if this has always been done, and in most cases it is unnecessary with 'guns' who have shot a good deal. But, depending upon the field of view in front of certain butts, it is occasionally very necessary indeed.

Now a 'gun' who is 'getting on a bit' is often deaf, especially if he has done a lot of shooting. And this deafness usually takes the

Driven grouse are probably the most difficult birds in the world to shoot; they can also be the most dangerous

form of a loss of the high notes. In short, a whistle denoting that the beaters are getting within range will be inaudible to him unless blown pretty close to his butt. It is clearly foolish to issue information that will not be heard: it may become dangerous if it is thought that such information has been received, when in fact it has not. I have known a good shot at the end of the day to be completely unaware that any signal concerning the proximity of the beaters had ever been given. People who are deaf do not like admitting it, and if they never hear the whistle are not likely to complain. I suggest that a horn blown as a warning is preferable.

The other point, touched on before, concerns swinging through the line. Criminal, of course, and never done by experienced 'guns'. But I believe it is in fact done a good deal more often than we like to think. Everybody knows that a grouse approaching between the butts must not be shot too close to the line. It is made the more dangerous, of course, because the movement of the gun when taking it is inevitably towards one's neighbour. The older 'gun', of whom I am talking, knows this better than most. He also perhaps has a subconscious feeling that his reactions may be slowing down a trifle. He may not be sure of this, but he is playing safe; he therefore lifts his gun in plenty of time to let the bird go through the line, so that he can shoot it behind.

Now here is the danger! By lifting the gun too soon, it is very easy – almost by instinctive timing – to get on to the bird again before it is through the line. The line of butts in one's mind's eye can quite easily be lost when concentrating on the bird; there is in addition the feeling that one can point to a bird behind the line a bit sooner, since the movement of the bird is taking the muzzles away from one's neighbour.

The result in the end is that someone in the line is shot, and shot too by a 'gun' who is confident that he is absolutely safe. The man who does fire such a shot is virtually always certain in his own mind that he did not fire until the bird was well through the line: and all sorts of theories are then advanced about shot ricocheting off birds or stones at extraordinary angles. But, whatever the theories, I believe that sometimes the shot was dangerous, and for the reasons I have advanced.

Good discipline: all the guns are ready, but all are pointed safely to the front and 'up in the air', except in the case of the man actually taking the shot

Now that I have become aware of this, it can be instructive (and frightening sometimes) to watch men, even those who have shot grouse for years, when they take a bird behind. Unless you are a 'class' shot (of whom there are remarkably few), there never seems to be enough time in a grouse butt. The bird through the line is going away, and you think you have to hurry to shoot it. And hurrying can be dangerous.

In short, I believe that it is quite often the bird taken behind that can lead to an accident. Even men who have shot a lot of grouse then sometimes fire a dangerous shot. I have seen it done! And though it *may* be a ricochet, it is not always so.

Here is a danger from an unexpected angle. To be forewarned about this is surely worthwhile, however much experience one may have.

At the shoot

All of us have our failings on the shooting field, but because we are but human, it is always the 'other chap' who does the silly things that can annoy us if we let them. There are many habits which I think can be reviewed. We shall recognise them at once in other people, but let us make quite certain that we are not guilty, too.

Do we always arrive on time? By 'on time', I mean ready to move off at the appointed moment with gun assembled, cartridges there, and boots on. We know the man who is always late – invariably with good reason – and then has forgotten something as well. I can indeed think of one young man whom we discussed as we waited. We wondered what he would have forgotten when eventually he did turn up. It was his gun.

Some of us are shy, and may be nervous of approaching a newcomer or guest (who is almost certain to be early): and yet if we are shy, how much worse must it be for the stranger. We are all a bit nervous at the beginning of the day, and this feeling is transmitted, without any doubt at all, to all dogs.

Dogs! Dogs out shooting can interfere with a day for everybody and wreck it for their owner. Even so, I have always

The dog which is the apple of its owner's eye can be the cause of much unnecessary delay and fuss

maintained that even the wildest brutes are less trouble than the average lot of 'guns'. Dogs are often obedient, out to please and enjoy themselves, and sometimes are intelligent. Some 'guns' have clearly not been granted any of these attributes.

Dogs really fall into two categories: those that are the apple of their owner's eye, and those that are not. The latter usually cause less bother; it is the former that drive the average host to the edge of insanity. It starts in the Land Rover. The pet has hopped in before the owner. It is promptly hauled out, given a lesson in sitting, and then told to get in after master is in. If the dog has any intelligence, this last command is not obeyed. The time it takes and the delay it causes is enormous; yet this is never remotely appreciated by the proud owner.

I must mention one other factor which arises with this breed. Nearly everyone knows that it is undesirable to talk when near

The result of anxious planning by host and keeper

game, as the human voice will frighten. This presumably does not count when summoning one's dog: the din thus created would be acutely embarrassing to the owner if he could hear himself as others hear him.

I have shot for a season or two with a friend who, when walking to his grouse butt, keeps up an almost continual yell at his far-ranging dog. The only time I have subsequently had a good drive is when I was No 1 and he was No 8.

The other breed of dog is scarcely noticed by its owner, and when missing is no worry provided it is not wrecking the next drive. It normally returns in due course with a hen pheasant – which has probably not even been shot at – and is then praised for its 'nose'. I have, of course, no need to write of the obedient, well-trained dog, just as I have no need to mention the same type of 'gun'. But human beings out shooting have their faults, too.

First there is the know-it-all. How often do we listen to one 'gun' who knows a great deal better than anyone else how to carry out a particular drive: certainly better than his host and his keeper, who have probably spent anxious hours planning the day, and have a good deal more expert knowledge. I recall a large private shoot which turned itself into a syndicate with paying 'guns'. I listened to one 'expert gun' describing how the previous drive should have been carried out, citing as his reason the fact that the bag was a good deal lower than it had been when it was a private shoot. What he did not realise (and still does not) was that only good shots were invited privately.

The gossip is kindly, generous and friendly, although usually 'getting on'. He will stop and talk in a most happy way with everyone. Unfortunately, he is often unable to remember his peg number, and when told will have the greatest difficulty in locating it. This will naturally involve the opportunity of a talk with each 'gun' and picker-up between where he has been helped out of the Land Rover and his proper position. He has no idea that his laborious progress does not help the 'guns' with whom he is talking when the birds are already coming – and neither does the fact that his own position is unoccupied.

When in addition he owns a dog of the 'apple-of-his-eye' variety, you lose one drive during the day.

Then there is the poor shot who explains to you why he is shooting so badly. Be very kind to him, though; listen patiently, even offer praise if this is possible. He is going through hell and of course it can so easily happen to you. If it does, do remember that it takes an awful lot of really dreadful markmanship before it is remarked upon.

The man who really makes you feel inferior is the one who turns up in a claret-coloured Rolls Royce, and then has someone to fit his pair of Purdeys together. If he offers you a drink at 9.30 am, take it: it will steady your nerves, and, if the truth were known, his own as well. For such splendid people often cannot shoot as well as their shop window might suggest.

The chap to beware of is that small unobtrusive man with a couple of well-behaved dogs. If you are a stranger, he is instantly kind, talking to you as if you were the most experienced shot there. He seems to know everyone, and the keepers and the beaters appear to know him much better than anyone else. Perhaps a local friend offered a day out? Except that he does not seem to miss much, and that after the first drive he presents as *your* bird one that you 'tinkered' and he finished off. It is only after lunch that someone tells you that he is the legendary 'John Smith', probably the best shot in the south of England, and was shooting at Sandringham the day before. But you can usually tell: he alone will remember his peg number after lunch.

Are we all as co-operative, helpful, polite and friendly as these real experts? I fear not, but we can always try.

Etiquette

In shooting, as in every other activity, custom has evolved rules for those taking part. Such rules always evolve to make life agreeable for those actually engaged in the activity. As ever, these rules become known as 'things that are done' and 'things that are not done'.

Non-compliance with these rules – which, I repeat, have been evolved for the enjoyment and safety of those taking part – results in less enjoyment for the rule-breaker; or indeed perhaps in no shooting at all, which means downright misery. So it is as well to know how to behave.

Nearly all the rules are dictated by good manners, common sense and the requirements of safety. Here are some of the rules.

Safety. Vital always. See the earlier section on this.

Talking. Do not. I do not mean ordinary social gossip when you are nowhere near game. But when you are waiting for or approaching game, *keep quiet.*

I once belonged to a syndicate of which one member was an incurable chatterer – and he had a rasping voice. I used to get all the shooting; after a bit, it became so noticeable that I was asked about it. I never let on, but all I did was *to keep away from the chatterer* – well away, the other side of the wood if I could. He never got much shooting, and neither did those near him.

Don't talk when waiting for the birds or when walking up; and this includes not talking to the lovely girl friend. And it also means not yelling at your dog. The human voice frightens game and game will not come near you, or your companions.

I sometimes had to arrive late at a shoot where there was plenty of land. I could always find the 'guns' because I could hear them chattering half a mile away. If I could hear them, certainly the game could. And those 'guns' still cannot understand why they saw plenty of birds on Friday when wandering around by themselves, and never much on Saturday when they were shooting together.

Invitations. Accept or refuse at once. Your host wants to know, because if you cannot go, he wants to get someone else. It makes it difficult for him, and indeed makes him appear impolite by having to give short notice, if you delay your decision.

When you have accepted, you *must* stick to it – particularly if a better invitation comes along later for the same day.

Arriving on time. If you are asked for 9.30 am, this really does mean that you must be ready to move off then. Arrive at 9.15 am so that you have time to get your boots on, gun out of its case and so on, to be ready at 9.30.

Being helpful to your host. If dogs are often quite undisciplined and unruly, they are nothing compared to the average group of 'guns'. One host used to say quietly once, 'Guns this way,' and then walk off. For the first two drives he had the shoot of his life, because none of the others were in position. They had not been polite enough to listen to their host. They were gossiping away, and just did not hear him – and so missed some very good shooting. After that they listened – as they should have done from the start.

Listen for your host's wishes, and be the first to comply. Why should he have to struggle to get the 'guns' moving and get the shoot started?

When you are in position, keep an eye again on your host – like a good cricket fielder watching his captain. If you are on a flank, and birds are breaking back, it simplifies your host's task if he can simply (and silently) wave you into a better position. But on no account move without his instructions.

Be helpful to your host. Volunteer for the 'walking gun', the outside berth when walking up and so on. It is, at the least, good manners. And (between you and me) you get more shooting that way too!

Cartridges. Take enough! It is sheer bad manners to run out of cartridges; it merely implies that you thought your host could only provide a limited supply of game – certainly less than he *did* – and this is scarcely complimentary. And fancy saving up half-days and all the rest to go shooting, and then seeing birds sail over your head unshot-at!

I remember one shoot when I remarked before I arrived, 'I expect we'll get five shots between us all day' – and the bag was 153 pheasants. I had enough cartridges and it was a splendid day – but supposing I had only taken enough for five shots!

Looking after your gun and equipment. Clean and oil your gun the same day as you fire it. There is a temptation, on coming back tired, to 'leave it until after your bath'. And we all know that it does not then get cleaned. And what about your boots too? Less valuable possibly than your gun, but liable to be ruined slightly quicker. *Neglect will ruin anything.*

158

Numbering. At some shoots – usually the super ones – you draw a number. The number you draw is the number of your butt or peg for the first drive. Usually, though not always, you number from the right, and your host will tell you how many guns 'you are numbering'. You usually move up two after each drive.

Let us suppose you draw No 1. At the first drive, you will be the right-hand 'gun'; for the next drive, No 3; then No 5, then No 7, and after that No 1 if 'numbering' eight guns. You add two on to each figure after each drive, so that No 8 becomes No 2 and so on. Remember what your number is for the first drive after lunch; this is too difficult for most people.

There are variations. Some shoots number from the left, so No 1 is the left-hand 'gun'. If you have seven guns, No 6 becomes No 1 and No 7 becomes No 2.

I heard of one shoot where 'guns' were told that odd numbers moved *up*, and even numbers moved *down* – two places each time. This was so complicated that everybody had a card with his number for each drive. I imagine it was done to give each 'gun' a different neighbour at each drive. Sort of Paul Jones – rather friendly.

Tipping. In an age of rapid inflation, it is well-nigh impossible to say how much. Before World War I, a grasping keeper knew the 'guns' who were guests as 'sovs' or 'half-sovs', depending solely on whether they would tip him £1 or 10s. It is a sobering thought that to be regarded as in the 'sov' class today you would have to tip about £20. We can only deduce that a keeper's income from tips has fallen in terms of real money very considerably.

Give as much as you reasonably can; and, above all, when you give it, show your appreciation for all the work he has put in.

Beaters and stops. Make friends with them! They are very nice people to know. They know more than you – or indeed most of the other 'guns' – about what is going on. They also know who are the good and safe shots, and who are not. Their opinion on the day is worth having; their opinion of you and your shooting

159

(*left*) Do not leave your gun where it can be knocked over by dog or man

(*centre*) Do not leave your gun where you can forget it as you drive off . . .

(*below*) . . . and you will not always see it if you leave it here!

has been likened to the sort of report which would be received if the Admiralty, for example, got an opinion on a senior officer from a junior officer serving under him. A bit of an eye-opener, we all suspect.

Hares. If you shoot a hare, carry it yourself if you are walking up or 'walking gun'.

Enjoyment. Be philosophical if you shoot badly — so easy to write, so very difficult to achieve. Do not excuse yourself if you have not shot well; probably no one has noticed, and certainly no one is interested! Keep your mouth shut if you are shooting well — everyone *will* have noticed. Congratulate good shooting; congratulate the poor shot on any good shot he has achieved — this is most heartening to someone who will almost certainly be depressed, and he may do the same for you one day.

Enjoy it!

Beaters and stops. They know more than most about what is going on — and who is hitting the birds!

6 Shotgun Coaching

General methods

To teach something well is rewarding. When you can actually see the successful results of what you are saying, it can be extremely satisfying. The big advantage of teaching shotgun shooting is that your pupil has come to you voluntarily, and is therefore on your side – to start with anyway! Thus it is obviously easier than teaching at school, where the pupil would probably not be there if he or she could help it, and even when in the classroom is not always 'with you' mentally.

Your task is to convey what you are trying to teach in a simple and comprehensible way. There are problems here: what is simple and clear to you is by no means always clear to your pupil. Indeed on occasion I have felt that some men do not comprehend the difference between up and down or push and pull. Nevertheless, it is up to you to make certain that your man does realise what you are endeavouring to put across.

There are men who in their own minds do exactly what you tell them to do. They then – although they conceal it very often – just do not believe you when you tell them that they are still doing it incorrectly. For example many people, when mounting their gun at an approaching bird, lift the butt too quickly with the right hand in order to get it into their shoulder, and this causes the muzzles to drop down – very often a long way down. Obviously this makes it difficult to get the barrels back 'on' again to any bird, because they now have so far to catch up.

Explain this and you will be understood. The grown man – determined not to dip his barrels – will often in fact do almost exactly as before. You tell him so again, and are not believed.

I evolved the idea of holding the whip aerial of my walkie-talkie close under the barrels from behind, so that if the barrels

The pupil has come to you voluntarily, and is therefore on your side – to start with anyway!

dipped on mounting they would hit the aerial. When this duly happened, I was at once accused of flipping the aerial up to make the pupil raise the barrels. None so blind as those who won't see!

This is the blacker side of the job. But do not think therefore that shotgun coaching is not rewarding to both pupil and instructor. It is! I repeat that in few teaching professions can you actually see the happy result of your instruction taking place before your very eyes. Sometimes one very simple phrase will be all that is needed. 'Hold your left hand further out on the barrels.' The result was immediate: a kill every time, instead of a miss. The 'gun' in question considered it nothing short of miraculous, which it was not. It was merely correcting the slightly faulty technique of a good shot. But it is this sort of thing that makes it all so worthwhile: shotgun coaching thus becomes an absorbing hobby.

Perhaps even more rewarding is teaching the young. They listen to what you say (as opposed to 'grown-ups', who, as I have said, sometimes do not); they have no bad habits to eradicate, and they are quick to learn. In fact I always maintain that a teenage boy quickly becomes a better shot than his father, however long Dad may have been shooting, unless father is a really first-class shot in the first place.

It is the experienced 'very average shot' who can be the most difficult to teach. If he has shot for a long time in a certain way, it is folly to pull that method to pieces in order to teach him the correct and simple method: he will simply revert to his old and faulty technique in moments of excitement.

Tell your pupil how to do it, and he will consistently hit his birds, provided you are there 'jogging his elbow', so to speak. At least, for a short time he will have seen the light, and perhaps realised how simple it all can be.

Burning it home

I believe there are three reasons why the 'average shot' never goes to a shooting instructor for help. It is too expensive; the instructor, he thinks, will try to give him a totally new technique which will probably destroy his present method; and finally, and most important, he is afraid that he will make a fool of himself.

Of course it is a bit expensive. One hundred cartridges are going to cost £8–£10, the clays another £4, and the instruction itself will vary from nothing to a considerable amount.

What do you get in return? I do not know of a single sport that initially can be performed easily by the 'common-sense' efforts of the human brain and body. It is true of shooting: one's initial approach to this sport is seldom the easiest way, and so it may take years of practice to get good results. Unlike the Edwardian landowner with ample income and time, we shall not be able to get the practice we thus need, so we may well be doomed to mediocrity if we rely solely on our own efforts. To put it another way, the good instructor can provide a very short cut to becoming a very good shot.

(*opposite*) A common mistake: the 'gun' does not put his butt firmly into his cheek and shoulder when he fires

'But so-called expert instruction will pull down all I have built up,' you may say. I must state categorically that unless you have a style of shooting that prevents you from ever hitting anything, this contention just does not hold water.

I am going to take a very simple example of a not unusual mistake: the 'gun' does not put his butt firmly into his cheek and shoulder when he fires. In rifle-shooting parlance, as I have written, he is in effect using an altered backsight every time he fires, with disastrous results on his accuracy.

The 'gun' is of course quite unconscious of this mistake, which, without expert advice, can cause endless confusion. For example, by not mounting his gun into his cheek, he shoots to the left. He receives unmistakable evidence of this by killing a grouse, let us say, to the left of the one he fired at. He decides to shoot in future a bit to the right, but next time by chance he mounts the gun correctly – and duly misses to the right. And, of course, over or under misses can also be managed in the same way, separately or at the same time. A good instructor can put this right in thirty seconds. Half a minute instead of years of frustration – surely cheap at the price!

'I am going to make a fool of myself before an expert.' I think this nonsense should be nailed right away. I am sure I am little different from many other teachers, and I realise that the pupil is almost certainly mentally playing an 'away match'. Indeed, I tell him so, and that I do appreciate this: and I rub it in that on no account must he be afraid of missing. 'This is the place to miss,' is what I tell everyone who comes for a bit of tuition.

Most people are indeed tense when they start the shooting lesson, so I always say that I am not going to comment on the first few shots. After that, it is usually easy to see what is going wrong. Let us suppose the pupil is mounting his gun badly. As I have said, I often take it away and tell him to position his hands and arms as if he were holding it. Then when the clay comes over, I tell him to point his left finger at the clay and keep on pointing at it as long as he can.

Now a man who is somewhat tensed up hears and absorbs only

a little of what you say. So I know for absolute fact that he will not remember to keep pointing at it! He will give a quick jab at it with his finger, and stop. I am ready for this, and he will get it at the second or third attempt. But it is simply not worth becoming annoyed if he does not do it right the first time: and if one gets a reputation for patience, it is entirely undeserved. It is simply knowledge that a comparatively tensed-up chap can take in only a very limited amount of information at a time.

It is uncanny, too, how quickly a man can forget. I realise this, and so, having told a pupil to mount his gun into his cheek and shoulder, I take great care to say 'Cheek and shoulder' just before each subsequent clay comes over. He then has only about two or three seconds to forget, which I may say is sometimes sufficient! But clearly he cannot go on shooting for ever with an instructor whispering the magic words before every shot. So what to do?

I ask him whether he has got and absorbed this bit of advice. The answer is invariably 'Yes'. So I tell him that I am going to give him ten shots on his own. I then try gently to rattle him by pushing in a cartridge quickly and pressing the buzzer for the next bird before he is quite ready. Inevitably, after about the fourth shot, he will revert: the gun will not be in his cheek and shoulder and he will miss. In the midst of this shooting, I say 'Cheek and shoulder,' quite loudly. He realises at once, and hits the rest of the clays. I have given him a sharp correction in the very act of his making the mistake that he normally used to make, and which he thought he had eliminated. Like the dog pulled up and corrected in the very act of running in, he is often cured for ever.

If this is too drastic, another simple technique can be adopted to drive home a simple correction which otherwise could be forgotten in the excitement of actually shooting. I tell the man I am going to distract him, so that unless he has really absorbed the simple correction that he has just successfully achieved for a number of shots he will revert and make the mistake again. He knows of course that he will not.

I then shout 'Over, over, *over!*' in a rising tone of voice before pressing the buzzer for the clay. When the clay then comes to him, he will miss because he has become excited and forgotten the correction. It is so ludicrous that we both usually burst out laughing: the fact that three shouted words, which he knows on reflection to be quite irrelevant, have actually caused him to forget the simple lesson of a moment before, is almost incredible. But the point is that he is now forewarned: however excited he gets when actually out shooting, this incident will come back to him and he will remember.

The art of teaching shooting is to ensure that a man will shoot well when you are not there to 'hold his hand'. Time after time, a man will receive instruction to his great advantage – at the time! But he will revert and fail if he does not, after receiving that advice, practise what he has been taught. And how many people do practise what they have been taught? Virtually none, I suspect. In short, a lesson has to be burnt home at the time, in order that it may have lasting benefit.

Of course, this applies to the man who is basically a good shot, but is making a comparatively simple mistake. If on the other hand he has to learn a more fundamental technique – to mount smoothly with the bird, for example – rather more gentle means may have to be employed. It is very difficult for a man to do something smoothly if he thinks he has not got enough time to do it at all. The average man mounts his gun anything but smoothly.

The fact that, if he does do it without jerking, he then has more time to shoot, is naturally beyond the realms of credibility: it is for this reason a waste of time to tell him so, and another method must be employed. I have an imaginary character that I now employ – a mythical Duchess of Lee, taken I regret to say from a somewhat ribald naval song. I paint her as a very haughty beauty sitting aloof in an eighteenth-century drawing-room. 'How,' I ask, 'would you approach her, if you wanted to dance the minuet with her? With a graceful bow, a sweep of the plumed hat, an elegant and gracious manner? Or just walk up and say

I am a great believer in getting a laugh from the pupil

"Ow about it, ducks?" Which approach is more likely to be successful?' And then I add, 'And which method have you been employing for the last few shots?' I can now insist on an elegant mounting of the gun, and the pupil finds to his astonishment that not only does he hit the clay, but he has more time in which to do it!

I am all the time trying to get my teaching across, and so I am a great believer in the laugh from the pupil. Most schoolboys are lazy, and of course you can tell this at once with the clever boys, however hard they are trying. I just tell them, after a stupid mistake involving something I have told them a minute before, that I sympathise with the masters at their school, who I bet enjoy their holidays. The idea that the masters might be glad to get rid of them – even temporarily – is so bizarre that they will laugh; and then they will do what I am trying to tell them.

It all sounds easy when writing about it, and indeed reading it. Every reader will see himself as the ideal pupil – easy to teach, amenable to suggestion, and improving rapidly as he grasps at once the merest hint of a suggestion. But I have yet to meet this paragon.

I am painting, I fear, a rather gloomy picture of the average man who comes to be taught. This is quite unintentional, and indeed would be a false picture. After all, the average pupil who comes to a shotgun instructor is obviously keen on shooting, which endears him to me: he wants to learn, and I enjoy teaching him. What a super combination for the acquisition of knowledge! What can be the difficulties in this perfect set-up?

What I am really saying is that many intelligent human beings unfortunately have a built-in resistance to learning, however hard they are trying: you have only to ask any schoolmaster, who will at once agree. One of the snags, as I have suggested, is that the pupil – especially if he is clever and has some shooting experience – simply does not listen; or perhaps, to be more polite, does not hear what you are saying. May I give another example? After a shot, I say to him, 'You were just astern of that one: all you have to do is to mount with the bird, and you will hit him right in the centre of the pattern.' As he says, 'Right. I've got the idea,' you can feel him saying to himself, 'Astern? OK, I'll give the next one a bit of lead.' You *know* this for fact! He has not heard what you said after you told him he was behind with the last shot. His mind leaps ahead, and he puts forward to himself the obvious but erroneous solution. I do not very often ask him what I have just told him, but when I do the reply is always, 'Just astern, wasn't it?' and then rather a shamefaced giggle about not quite catching the rest.

One further point. Any man under instruction is only capable of absorbing, and then carrying out, one thing at a time. If, for example, he is looking at his gun as he mounts, and not putting the butt properly into his cheek and shoulder, it is beyond human ability to correct both these mistakes at the next shot. I tackle this problem by saying, 'Look at the bird only for the next shot. I don't care whether you hit or miss: concentrate on this only.' I then encourage as hard as possible, even if he continues to miss, until he has got the 'looking at the gun' mistake eliminated. Then and only then can I correct the 'cheek and shoulder' error.

In essence then, the task of teaching the average man to shoot well is comparatively easy. I know this for I have taught many people in a day, and the vast majority of these were shooting well – at comparatively easy 'birds', admittedly – at the end of ten shots.

At the end of it all, it must be realised that if it is thrilling for the pupil to start hitting them as well as understanding how he is doing it, it is quite soul-satisfying to the instructor. It really boils down to the fact that each pupil should try to get all he possibly can out of the chap who is teaching him. This is what I tell all the people who come to me.

Coaching for clay pigeon clubs

More and more clay pigeon clubs are starting up. This is because the sport of shooting is becoming more and more popular, and since we are not all landowners, often the only way that a beginner can get any shooting at all is to shoot clays. Although established clay pigeon clubs are expanding their membership, it is I think the new clubs that are producing the greater number of 'new boys'. And it is sometimes these clubs that make mistakes to start with.

Let us see what so often happens in a new club. As it is 'obviously' a waste of time to have easy shots, the clays are thrown in such a way that they are difficult because of angle and distance, or because of the lack of time available for the shot. For the average beginner, a hit is not more and no less than a fluke.

All this sounds as if experienced members are totally unsympathetic to the beginner. On the contrary, they are almost always out to help. Unfortunately, it is lack of experience in teaching that does the harm.

Nearly anybody can see that the beginner is, for example,

missing behind. Everybody tells him so, and for the next shot he is determined not to be astern. Unconsciously he tries to intercept by giving more lead, and with the gun quite stationary miles ahead of the target, he pulls the trigger, and misses – you know where. No one can see *why* he is missing behind, and their helpful advice is actually making things worse. For a man to persevere under these conditions requires a good deal of character and determination.

I believe that for every sport, whether it be tennis, shooting, singing, what you will, there is an established 'best way' of doing it. I must repeat that I believe that in virtually every case, this is *not* the natural or instinctive way adopted initially by most human beings. To shoot very well then needs a certain technique. This has got to be learnt, and thus the beginner must not be rushed, because his brain must have enough time in which to tell his unpractised muscles what to do. If you hurry him, his

Each pupil should try to get all he possibly can out of the chap who is teaching him

mind will forget. And if that is not enough, his muscles will then let him down, even when his mind is instructing them correctly. As long, therefore, as people tackle the sport of shooting without instruction, they will reach only a standard well below what they are capable of.

I believe that most clubs could improve the shooting of their members by getting a skilled instructor to help them. There are two difficulties: one is the cost, on which more in a moment, and the other is sometimes the experienced shot within the club.

The experienced man is nearly always embarrassed when at first instructed. He is frightened of missing, especially in front of others with whom he has a certain reputation of being above average. And if he does miss, it must obviously be the instructor who is making him do it! Great skill is here required from the instructor, but once he has got the confidence of the 'old hand' he can quickly turn him from an average shot who will never get any better into a very good shot who will.

And the beginner can be put on to the right course at once: as soon as he has got the basics right, any subsequent mistake can be quickly ironed out without having to start at fundamentals.

The junior member is the person most likely to benefit. (If you want the worst conceivable combination of instructor and pupil, get the average father trying to teach his son: no need to elaborate on this!) Why not start the young boy correctly? —Why not indeed: except that he will quickly be better than Dad.

Now the cost. It can of course be very high, for an experienced coach has a skill that is not easily bought. But spread across all the members, it should not be too expensive. And there are some very skilled men who will be anxious to help anyone who is keen, and will ask little more than expenses. Good luck to them and you.

Finally, I believe that instruction of the sort I advocate is of even more value to the club than to an individual. The cost will probably be lower, and the members can compare notes afterwards. In fact, some of the best shots living have started just like this.

Coaching at game fairs

'It takes all sorts . . .,' they say. And this is certainly illustrated when you set out to coach all comers at shooting at a game fair. It may seem odd that anyone will spend quite a lot of money to have ten shots or so, and think that this is enough to learn how to shoot – yet surprisingly enough, it often is!

It is of course decidedly encouraging and exciting for the spectators to see a pupil miss a couple of clays, receive a quiet word from the instructor and perhaps a moment of demonstration, and then produce a succession of hits, accompanied by an excited grin. I have actually experienced a round of applause from the audience, directed at a young beginner who had shot remarkably well and indeed had not missed a clay. As I had told him that I was not particularly pleased at his hitting the clays, but far rather at his doing it the right way, this young man I believe had his day made for him.

I recall one boy of eleven who shot absolutely correctly for the first three shots. I then asked him who had been coaching him, and he replied simply, 'Me Dad.' I turned round to the crowd to see who it might be, and was rewarded by the sight of a man with a grin stretching from ear to ear. No need whatever to ask who was the proud father!

There is, of course, another side to the picture: for instance the man who 'has not shot for a bit', who as soon as he grasps the gun shows that he has never shot even a little bit. Perhaps the most difficult to deal with is the experienced man who just wants 'tuning up a bit'. Very often, unfortunately, he is self-taught, and complains with good reason that he is never consistent. There is an appalling temptation to teach him only to hit the clays. What do you do? Teach him to hit them? Easy! He will be grateful and will depart certain that he has 'got it', although we all know that he has not and never will at that rate. Try to show him the right way, and he will leave convinced that you have wrecked his shooting for ever.

Sometimes a man comes forward who is – to use a naval

174

expression – so 'kack-handed' that he finds it difficult to mount his gun anywhere near the target. He is often a highly intelligent being, frequently left-eyed, and can be recognised immediately by his gleaming knuckles as he holds the gun. I am almost surprised that the fore-end of his weapon has not the imprint of his left hand driven in upon the wood, so tight is his grip. Kindness alone suggests that somehow – never mind how – such a man must be induced to hit one clay at least.

But usually the penny drops, and a man will realise that here is revelation: that it is indeed simple, and that a simple method really does make it all easy. Such a pupil, who tells *you* how it is all dropping into place, is of course intensely satisfying.

Instruction soon falls into a sort of routine. Get the pupil to stand correctly with the gun at the 'ready' position pointing roughly in the direction from which the target will come. This does not take long. Next tell him to mount the gun at the top of a tree or hedge. Very often, if he has watched previous pupils, he will do this correctly. Next I give him a couple of 'mounts' at a clay with the gun unloaded. Then the first shot: if he is mounting correctly, there is an 80 per cent chance that he will hit and hit correctly. If he does not, I ram home the fact that here is the place to miss, where it doesn't matter – and that he is really learning when he does miss. It is not long before he is hitting them regularly and correctly.

Schoolboy coaching

As a boy and a young man I was given very great encouragement to shoot by an uncle who lived in Norfolk. As a direct result, I have enjoyed shooting in all sorts of places over much of the world. In short, this man gave me a great deal of pleasure through his original encouragement.

If this is true of me, surely it will be true of boys and young men of today. How then can we give this same encouragement and help to those young people who would perhaps like to shoot?

What I suggest is that clay pigeon clubs up and down the

I suggest that clubs start schoolboy days

country should start schoolboy days or evenings. These can be expanded into schoolboy matches, and perhaps the club (or a member) could be persuaded to present a schoolboy cup.

It is necessary to circulate members to find out whether they have suitable children, or whether they know of any young boys who might be interested. A sympathetic coach will also be needed: such a person may not exist within the club, and it will then be necessary to contact a professional. I have always believed that the best teachers of shooting in the world are the recognised coaches in the London shooting schools. Although I have not met all of them, the coaches at other shooting schools in the rest of England are undoubtedly of the same standard.

I do not know whether the top gunmakers could spare one of their coaches in, say, the spring to come up for a weekend of such coaching: I can only say that a London gunmaker of the very top rank has helped us in the past a great many times. The actual cost would be high, but if the club subsidised the venture, and father paid a nominal amount, it should not be ruinous.

I suggest that boys should be coached in pairs – that is, two every hour. Over a weekend, something like thirty-five to forty boys could be coached at a fee of about £3 each. The sum thus collected would help to make the fee charged even by top London gunmakers seem not too bad. The coach has to be a dedicated man to achieve this number, but of course, all shotgun coaches *are* dedicated men!

If you have not enough schoolboys, why not fill up with a few adults? They will need it, especially since their sons, with a bit of coaching of this standard under their belts, will rapidly begin to outshoot them. It is of course much harder work to coach a grown-up; or, put the other way round, to coach a youngster is comparatively easy, and some boys rapidly become extremely good shots. I have said it before, but I must repeat that it is a most rewarding thing – indeed thrilling – to see a small boy shooting well as a result of being well taught. Perfection in miniature! They never look as if they will miss. They are hitting clays with a ·410 which their fathers would miss clean with their 12-bores. They will never be bad shots as long as they live. They have been taught the right way to shoot at an age when they can easily absorb correct instruction. It is an opportunity that must not be missed. They are taught safety when actually shooting and so learn it quickly. And of course they are meeting contemporaries who, with any luck, will shoot with them for the rest of their lives.

It can help the clay pigeon club too, of course, because schoolboy coaching of this nature has, for some reason, a good deal of publicity value. The local paper will almost certainly send a photographer and will write up the event, and local television or radio may also cover it if given sufficient notice. It is difficult for the media to make mock of this sort of thing: in their eyes, you are not killing anything. The reporter and the photographer may not be very enthusiastic countrymen, but if offered the chance they will undoubtedly be keen to 'have a go'; it is not beyond the bounds of possibility that they may get 'hooked', and you will have another enthusiastic member or two on your hands! And, of course, more than your fair share of good reporting.

A schoolboy match is also fun. Two fathers who preferably live some way apart might be asked to form opposing teams. Tell them both at the same time, because they will be ruthless at pinching the best boy shots wherever they come from. (If you are one of the fathers, tell the other father *after* you have picked your team – for the same reason!)

There are two requirements for success. One is a coach – or at least, someone who can see the shot – to coach all members of both teams impartially. It is most distressing if a small boy, consumed with nervousness, does not hit a single clay – quite enough to put him off for a long time. The other requirement is a very heavy tea afterwards.

If we are in a position to encourage the young but do nothing about it, I believe that we are being selfish. Some of us can indeed provide encouragement for the younger generation, and I hope I have shown briefly how this can be done.

7 Out Shooting

Types of game

Grouse are smaller than pheasant and larger than partridge, which they resemble. They are sometimes found singly, but more often in groups or coveys of up to twenty birds. Later in the season they often pack in large numbers.

They feed mostly on heather shoots, and occupy the lonely and sometimes bleak moors in the north of England and in Scotland. They exist virtually nowhere else in the world. Grouse have to be hardy, in view of the cold hard conditions in which they live, and indeed they are so tough that even in these unfavourable conditions they breed and mature early. They can take to their wings within a week of hatching, and in spite of an endemic disease on every moor they are among the strongest birds that fly. They may be shot from 12 August – earlier than any other game bird – until 10 December.

It is always possible to learn something about grouse shooting, if you are young and active, by going beating. Beating in pheasant shooting means what it says – you beat through the woods. In grouse driving, beating means long hours of walking through heather in glorious surroundings: this is rewarding in terms of both health and enjoyment, and perhaps not without some financial advantage too. It will certainly show you what the sport of grouse shooting is all about, and prepare you for the day when you actually take part in the shooting. There is also always a demand for a man with a retriever to pick up behind the line.

If you have no other means of introduction, it is probably best initially to approach one of the agencies which advertise grouse shooting.

At one extreme of the sport, you might be one of eight or ten borne up to a paved butt by Land Rover on a sunny August day to have 200 or more grouse driven over you four or five times in the course of the day. At the other extreme, you can walk and scramble all day with a couple of friends and a dog and come home with two or three brace, blisters, and a huge appetite.

Whatever the image, a degree of endurance is required for shooting on the remote and rugged moors where the grouse live. In October or November, in the cold and perhaps in a gale, you have to be fit if you are to last the day. Grouse shooting is not for the lazy or cossetted individual.

There are two methods of shooting grouse: by walking up or by driving. When walking up, pointers are sometimes used. These dogs will 'point' at grouse concealed in the heather, and show the 'gun' where to go. When the grouse gets up, he shoots. This is not quite as easy as it sounds, for the bird is elusive and your heart can be thumping with exhaustion and excitement. Walking up can only be done early in the season because the grouse quickly become wild and will rise out of shot.

Driving is different, the birds being 'pushed' by beaters towards the 'guns', who will be standing in butts (i.e. hides). Distances – to a townsman – are enormous: a drive can be two miles in length, with the beaters frequently out of sight until the end of the drive.

Men come from all over the world to shoot grouse. Grouse shooting has a thrill which cannot be denied; indeed it is to many people the most exciting form of shooting that exists.

The *pheasant* is a noble bird said to have been 'imported' to Britain by the Romans. It is surprisingly self-sufficient and will survive under difficult conditions – though American GIs armed with rifles took a heavy toll of the species during World War II. It is now bred and 'conserved', ostensibly for shooting purposes, though if this were not done the pheasant would by now have virtually disappeared from our countryside. It likes a warm wood, but will survive in marsh and hedgerow.

It is a bird not without cunning, and as it gains experience will use its legs to escape rather than flying. The human voice gives splendid warning, and those with eyes to see will notice many birds making for safety before the 'guns' are even in position.

The pheasant shooting season starts on 1 October – 'when the leaves are off the trees' – but early in the season the shooting is really limited to the hedgerows and root fields. This is not the best sport, although the pheasant is a strong bird and can lift itself almost out of shot extremely quickly – indeed altogether too quickly for some of us.

The real cream of pheasant shooting comes when the woods are driven out, with the 'guns' waiting in nervous anticipation. These birds may of course blunder out little more than head-high, in which case they are not shot at. But where it can be contrived the birds are sent over the 'guns' high in the air. A pheasant well up, curling in the wind and making for home, is nearly as safe as the proverbial house. And the 'gun' thus defeated will often raise his hat to an adversary that has clearly proved too good for him. Under these conditions, the odds are fairly on the bird, and it is a good shot who can feel pleased with himself after such a drive.

The *partridge* is a small bird which likes open country and a light soil. It almost always builds its nest in hedgerows, and of course increases in numbers when protected from vermin. There has in the last twenty-five years been a great decline in the number of these birds, largely owing to poisonous chemical fertilisers and the grubbing up of hedges. The days of the 'partridge manors' in Norfolk and Hampshire are probably gone for ever.

The partridge pairs for life, and its family may number as many as twenty. They will keep together, and fly as a covey. Early in the season they can be walked up on stubbles or in roots. This may sound easy shooting, but it is not so. A covey bursting into the air, sometimes almost from your feet, can be extremely disconcerting!

Later in the year, they are usually driven over the 'guns'. This requires great skill on the part of both keeper and beaters, and silence from the 'guns'. The human voice, as I have said, is a splendid warning: and partridges are not deaf.

All game birds have, in the words of the RAF, a 'high wing loading', and therefore have to fly fast. The partridge is no exception, and its rapid wingbeat makes it appear to fly faster than it actually does. A covey coming over the hedge and seeing the 'guns' will give what amounts almost to a start of surprise, and 'burst' in all directions. It requires among other things a cool head – there is a lot of space round a partridge coming over you – to shoot your bird.

Experience of driven grouse

Driven grouse are tough and unpredictable, the most difficult birds in the world to shoot – and probably, as I have suggested, the most exciting.

Grouse fly low, nearly always on a curve, and at the same time can rise or fall disconcertingly as they come towards you. They are comparatively heavy birds, and so have a high wing loading. And this means that they fly fast: they have to.

Oddly enough, what makes driven grouse so difficult to shoot is this fact that they fly low. It means that you have to shoot them in front of your butt or behind: to fire at them as they pass you would mean that you would shoot your neighbour. And of course you must not shoot in front when the beaters come in range. You think that there is very little time, and unless you are deliberate, you will *not* have enough time.

When I was first asked to shoot grouse, I was determined to do my best. I went to a shooting school, and fired a hundred cartridges at 'driven grouse'. My instructor was kind enough to say he was pleased with me. Full of confidence, I took myself to Scotland, and in due course into a butt.

The first lot came low, slightly to my left and not very fast. I swung on them exactly as I had been taught, and with complete confidence. Nothing happened at my two shots: not a bird had flinched. They ploughed past me with a strong wing stroke. They seemed to have come from nowhere, and were bound with determination for a far destination, and had not been deflected to the least degree from their purpose by me.

Thoughtfully I reloaded. It was not quite as easy as I had thought. There was quiet and peace. I relaxed. The day was warm, the scenery superb. The faint buzz of insects was almost soporific, and gradually my thoughts wandered. Suddenly I realised that the air around me was full of rushing dark shapes. I could hear the swish of wings through the air. Desperately I swung round, and fired the first barrel into a large space between a cloud of birds. With a great effort, I steadied on to the last bird and fired. It flew on – untouched, and apparently unaware that I had even fired.

What was I doing wrong? They were so different from the clay pigeons at the shooting school. There seemed so little time before the birds went into the danger arc, and there were so many that it was hard to choose which bird to take.

Ah! Here was another big lot to my left: I had at least seen them well out. As I watched them approach, two more birds flung over me from my right. I had not seen them until then, but I transferred my shallow allegiance to them in a flash as they flicked away behind me. Neither bird took the remotest notice of my shots. By the time I had reloaded, the big lot I had watched approaching had disappeared.

There appeared to be only one solution: I had not got any shot in my cartridges. I had actually got one cartridge in my teeth, determined to bite it open to see for myself, when suddenly I saw a grouse coming fairly high and fast towards me on my left. I put up my gun and fired. The grouse collapsed instantly and hit the front of the butt with a thump.

That at least demolished the theory concerning my cartridges. But it did not really solve the difficulty of hitting driven grouse. I was a good deal wiser at the end of my first grouse-driving day, and realised – unpalatable truth – that I was a pretty poor shot.

The truth of the matter is that driven grouse are very difficult indeed to hit consistently. You, as a 'gun', always seem to be playing an 'away match'. The surroundings, though superb, are strange; the bird comes at you like a swerving, unexpected cannon ball; you have a restricted arc in which you can shoot; and it is of course terribly exciting.

To shoot such birds successfully, you have got to keep your head; your shooting technique must be well-nigh perfect, and produced unconsciously; and you must be deliberate when every nerve is screaming for haste. A failure in any one of these categories means, at the least, a succession of misses. To achieve success in one category is hard enough; to achieve all at the same time is miraculous. But after your second or third drive, a bird will at least often swerve at your shot, instead of the previous utter indifference.

If you can learn to hit them, and hit them consistently, you will be able to shoot anything that flies. After a bit, you do begin to hit them. It is an art that can be learnt – indeed, it is the art of the possible, once you know how. The difficulty is to find someone who has mastered the business and who then has the ability to put his knowledge across, and of course you yourself must have the humility of spirit to absorb that knowledge and put it into practice.

The average pheasant shot will make nothing of them; a good partridge shot is scarcely likely at first to shoot his share. All, I think, will be appalled at their standard of marksmanship to start with. There are very few good grouse shots.

It is easy to emphasise the difficulty of shooting driven grouse. Not all of them are difficult; a few – though not many – are frankly easy. It is perhaps their unexpectedness as much as anything that causes one to miss.

If the grouse are expected from the 'obvious' angle – let us say from behind a small hillock to the left – they will in fact come from the right, where no beater (one thinks) could ever put up a bird. I have now adopted the habit, when I see a bird coming to my left, of giving a quick, automatic look to the other flank to see what is approaching from this direction. If you do not do this, you are certain to be surprised: and the bird that surprises you is a 'sitter' coming in on the opposite side. If you do carry out this drill, you are still surprised, but not quite so often!

The drives are long. Very often quite a number of birds will come over you early on. This means you will be caught napping, for you know that the beaters could not yet be in position. (They have, of course, put up these birds as they were walking to the start of the drive.) If this happens you will be on tenterhooks for the next twenty minutes, during which time nothing whatever will occur. Your concentration will slacken; and yet again you will be surprised.

Strangely, large numbers do not help. How often do you see a single grouse, twisting and turning towards a butt, fall dead to a single shot. On the other hand, how frequently can a mass of birds pour down on two butts, and not a feather be touched in spite of a hurried fusillade. It is much easier to concentrate on a single bird: a mass of birds enables you to select one bird, realise an instant later there is an easier one to the right, change your mind and miss them all. Everybody does it, and will continue to do so as long as grouse are shot at.

I suppose that this form of shooting is such fun because people are enjoying themselves so much that they cannot help becoming friendly. There is the good shot; usually the least obtrusive member of the party, who arrives in the least expensive car. You do not notice him until he starts shooting, and then his skill is obvious. He is patently safe; never seems to be in a hurry, and yet he is probably shooting quicker than you, for all your haste. He keeps his head – and that is saying something when the birds are really coming – and he kills an awful lot of birds. He always seems to get a little bit more than his share of the shooting.

And a poor shot can be an asset too. There is one I know who, after shooting badly himself, has the greatness of character to congratulate his neighbour on shooting well. There are admittedly not many men with sufficient Christian generosity to do this. But such humble great men do exist. And, just occasionally, a sort of divine influence comes upon such mortals, and for one drive at least they cannot miss. This is such a surprise to everyone, including themselves, that joy is unconfined. And although a valiant attempt is made to pretend that such skill is a fluke, no man born of woman could convince himself – let alone anyone else – that such really was the case in such circumstances. And anyway, he deserves his luck.

There are others, of course. The dangerous shot: nearly always well known, and nowadays often tolerated as rather a joke. 'Old George always gets someone once a season; two in a vintage year.' This view, however, is not accepted by anyone he has actually shot. Nor is it amusing to see your son, for example, standing in a butt with 'old George' next to him swinging down the line. When shooting driven grouse, it is very easy to be dangerous; even the most careful can sometimes fire a dangerous shot. It is the chap who does not care, or does not realise the potential danger who is bound to fire a dangerous shot sooner or later.

And then there is the talker. We have all met him: he usually has a disobedient dog, an amusing lady companion, and a carrying voice.

All this, however, is only a series of pinpricks in what is nearly always a lovely day. Even so, a day's grouse shooting can be pretty testing. Late in the year, it can be cold and snowing. The grouse are strong and apparently made of cast iron. Downwind – often a gale with some snow – they are practically untouchable. And when you do 'touch' them – you can nearly always hear the shot hit them – they are capable of displaying a splendid indifference. A good long wait in really cold weather in a butt near the clouds can be pretty unpleasant. You will not get a great many shots, but those you do will test you, or indeed anyone. And the birds you kill, you will not forget.

It is a sport that can give you both ecstasy and black depression almost simultaneously. I can still hear the instinctive cry of despair from my left-hand neighbour as he missed a real 'sitter'. He was, of course, unaware that he had opened his mouth, but I know how he felt. But after that, in the same drive, he got some splendid birds and the agony of the moment was forgotten. If it did nothing else, it made me realise that everybody who goes into a grouse butt may suffer despair. He may on the other hand be rewarded, and such a prize is worth gaining, for it will not come easily.

A good pheasant shoot

I did not know it, but it was to be one of the best days' shooting that I have ever had. Everything, as it occasionally does, went right from start to finish.

I had two guns with me, for I had been told that I would be 'lent' a loader. I had plenty of cartridges and it was a most beautiful November morning. The estate where I was shooting was a very large one, and we were shooting the home beat. It was nice to see old friends as I arrived, and I hurried to get on my boots and get my guns ready. My loader was the local policeman. He was the best loader I have ever had.

My host came towards me with a grin of welcome, and I drew my number. No 2 for the first drive, numbering from the left – quite a good position, and I knew the drive well. We stood in an avenue of very tall beeches on a road: opposite was a large straggly wood which usually held a lot of birds.

I was talking quietly to the policeman when we both saw a hen pheasant, high and to our right and just visible through the trees. She had the slight breeze under her tail, and was making for safety as soon as the drive had started. Almost instinctively I pushed my gun at her and pulled. The bird simply stopped flying, and hit the branches of the trees on the other side of the road with a crash. I broke the gun to reload, but the loader quietly took it from me, and I seemed to have the other gun in my hand without knowing it. As I grasped it, I heard a quiet 'Half left,' and there was another bird gliding through the trees, having got up a long way back. Again the gun came up smoothly, and I clearly heard the shot strike. The hen pheasant bounced off the road in a cloud of feathers. I slipped the safety catch on, and quietly changed guns. I was back where I had begun, but two birds were stone dead behind me before the drive had fairly started. With a loader like that, I reckoned that about all I would

187

have to do would be to pull the trigger.

The second drive promised to be a repetition of the first. Again the quiet 'Half left' from my loader, and I saw a cock pheasant coming high at me and getting higher. I hit the pheasant, and from that moment forgot all except shooting. I had the drive of my life.

We stopped for 'comforts'. My right-hand neighbour, who had not been shooting well, got there first, and he subsequently shot very much better. How difficult it is to achieve confidence when you begin with no confidence in yourself. Those who can manage this impossibility become great men – and almost certainly good shots too!

At the next drive, I was No 6, rather too far to the right to be in the centre of things. But since it was to be a day to remember, the beaters by mistake inclined a little too far to their left in the large wood they were driving, and the centre of the drive came over me.

I was surprised by a hen pheasant which had got up from the back of the wood and came straight over me very high and fast. I was quite confident about this really high bird – probably the only time I ever have been or ever will be. I pointed with the bird and fired. I can honestly say that on that day I expected the bird to collapse. Nothing happened. Still confident, I fired the second barrel: the bird sailed on without the slightest indication that I had ever fired my gun, let alone in her direction.

It sounds inconceivable, but I knew so well that things were with me on this day that the episode did not worry me. It was clear that that particular bird was safe that day, and nothing I or anybody else could do would alter that fact. My loader said nothing and neither did I.

There was a pause: I could just hear the beaters, and some pigeon, alarmed, flew up and out of the wood. I saw, even at this stage of the drive, an old cock creeping along the hedge in front of me, looking for a way out. There were a few hurried shots on the right – obviously a bird or two breaking back – and then more silence, except for a small bird or two calling. It was still, sunny and cold, but there was an air of tenseness as of things to come. Surely a tenseness of our own making: and yet perhaps not quite. Every bird in the wood – and there were many – must have known of danger, and was moving in the bushes, or perhaps already tucked into some piece of undergrowth. We waited.

There was a noise 'as of a moth fluttering in a matchbox' far in front, and a splendid cock pheasant rose. He topped the high trees in front, passed above us and set his wings as he curved away to my right, moving very fast over my neighbour. I offered up a short prayer that the 'comforts' had not died in him. He pointed the gun at this high curving bird and fired. The cock pheasant threw back his head, and seemed to go on falling for some time before he hit the turf a long way back. One 'gun' had had his day made.

The birds now began to come, and I and my loader were kept busy. I was still shooting well, for it was one of those days when I felt that it would be almost difficult to shoot badly.

There is an expression 'too much of a good thing'. We are always envious – at least I am – of the man who has as much money as he wants, or as much shooting as he can get, or indeed as much as he wishes of anything that we think desirable. And yet, when and if we get it, the savour seems to die. We quickly get sick of too much of anything. And so it was with me. I got tired of shooting the 'easy' bird and began to choose the difficult shot only. There were so many birds, and I was shooting so well, that probably for the only time in my life I could afford to do this.

We came to the last drive, and I was on the outside. I was not sorry, for I had had some wonderful shooting that day, and in any case I was on a slight rise and could see the other 'guns' shooting. I could see clearly from the angle of one gun that the shot was always behind the high birds; this was caused by the man 'checking' as his brain said 'Pull.' But there was one 'gun' in particular who was a beautiful shot – in quite a different class from the rest of us. It was not how much he killed, though this was impressive, but how he did it. It always seemed so easy: he had so much time, and the bird was always dead in the air. It was a very great pleasure to watch him at that drive.

I suppose no man is a hero to his loader, but the policeman was kind enough to say he had had a good day. I pretended to agree that it had been 'not bad', but I did not believe what I said: it had been the most wonderful day's shooting I had ever had in my life.

Reputation

There are some fortunate people shooting who acquire the reputation of being in the top flight as marksmen. Once such a reputation has been achieved, even though it is often an illusion, it is quite hard to lose it. I suppose on reflection that this is true of nearly all opinions about individuals, good or bad.

One factor that runs like a thread through it all is that a good reputation gets better and better with the telling. How often do we meet the man who has the reputation of being a good shot: although it may be gratifying to see him miss, anything he does kill is regarded at once as an example of what a really good performer can do.

Another interesting thing is that good shooting is always noticed and remarked upon, whereas poor shooting often is not. Perhaps because we unconsciously think that 'there, but for the grace of God, go I', we have a mental blockage when we see someone missing fairly consistently. And if we are envious of someone shooting better than ourselves, then perhaps we feel we can afford to be more generous to the chap who is 'off his day'. After all, he might do the same for us one day.

We must be clear that there is all the difference between being a good shot and merely having the reputation of being so. The good shot is by definition a good shot, and by that I mean that he kills a lot of birds in a day's shooting. Many of us consider that a man is a marksman if he kills one bird in two, yet it should not be by his average that a man is judged, but by what he kills.

I recall a 'gun' coming out of a grouse butt so pleased with himself that he could scarcely talk. He had killed twelve grouse – and, he added with what I fear can only be called smug satisfaction, 'with sixteen shots'. Well, this was not bad, and anybody would have been pleased, I think. But grouse had been pouring over his butt all through the drive, and a really good shot would have had thirty birds down with never mind how many shots.

The truth is that the really 'class' shot takes birds which most of us would never even attempt, and kills them. The quick one flicking away and only half seen – stone dead. The really high bird which so many people would claim quite sincerely as 'out of shot' – killed cleanly again and again. And the time he gives himself to kill his second bird!

How then does one get the 'good shot' reputation? First, I think, one must be at least an average shot – good enough to kill all the 'sitters' pretty often. Indeed, if you want to be considered almost a super shot, all you have to do is never to miss the easy ones; and, heaven knows, an awful lot of the birds at which you shoot are (in retrospect!) not too difficult.

Second, you must take advantage of your luck. As someone put it when asked how he'd got on: 'I wasn't really shooting up to my form.' He then paused, and continued: 'To tell you the truth, I never have.' But all of us, I believe, have days when the birds fall as if struck by a death ray. The actual demise of the birds need not be noticed, but the number of birds picked up should if possible for reputation's sake be remarked upon by a keeper or beater. They often have a shrewd idea of who is hitting them, and their gossip is considered quite unbiased. It is a certain boost to reputation, for instance, if a beater asks casually at the end of a grouse drive, 'How many?' and you can say 'Seventeen,' when the normal score is eight or nine. Nothing is known about the fact that you had all the shooting, that six at least were such 'sitters' that a boy of nine could have killed them, and that three times a bird at which you had fired flew on while the one next to it collapsed. No! You are quickly known as the chap who killed seventeen at such-and-such a drive. And it soon becomes twenty-seven. Beautiful shooting, they will tell you – though they were not even there!

191

If you have written an article or a book even faintly connected with the sport, you begin on any day with more than a head start, and it takes quite a lot of wretched shooting to destroy a reputation which you have achieved without the faintest justification. You have only to see the whites of a fellow sportsman's eyes, as he raises them in horror at the very thought of shooting next to someone who has actually written about it, to realise how much start you have already got in the reputation stakes.

A bit of luck helps here too. Once at a spaniel trial, someone mentioned at half-time that one of the guns had written such a book. There was a fortunate lack of interest, but after lunch three things happened. First, he killed a bird by a colossal fluke; second, someone else killed a bird, and even though the author had not even fired, everyone thought it was him; and finally, two pheasants got up quite well apart, and the bird at which he fired flew on, but the other fell as if struck by a hammer. It was at this point that one of the judges came over and enquired, '*Who* did you say your publisher was?'

There are people who will never be good shots in actual fact. With great perseverance and concentration, they can often manage to eliminate the grosser errors from their faulty techniques and become quite fair performers. Under certain conditions of fortune, they may even get a reputation far above their true worth. On the other hand, you occasionally find the man who has, perhaps by chance, adopted the correct technique for shooting at a moving target, and who is indeed a super shot – a true giant amongst pygmies. He is instantly recognised as such, without any need for luck.

One should not, I suppose, envy such mortals; but oh, how I sometimes wish and wish . . .

For ladies only, or how to marry a grouse moor

There may, I feel, be a need for advice to the pretty girl who wishes to marry a grouse moor – a very wise and laudable aim in life. First she should select her moor, and then engage his interest by the normal methods. 'How delightful,' he may say; 'I shall really look forward to tomorrow, if you can come with me in my butt.' But unless the lady is experienced as a shooting companion, all can be set for a pretty disastrous day. The basic difficulty, of course, is that any female likes to be taken notice of, and here are the seeds of discontent.

No attractive lady will like what I now have to say, but it is true: any man out grouse shooting will be thinking exclusively of two things, namely grouse and shooting. Occasionally a third party will intrude – his dog. Although good manners will no doubt sugar this pill a bit, any female finds it hard to believe that her partner of the evening before does not realise she is even there. She therefore instinctively sets out to attract attention.

Clothes come at once to the female mind: and true to her sex, she aims to be elegant. Now it is usually impossible to be truly elegant on a grouse moor. To start with the feet, shoes or boots must be practical. A light attractive shoe – however shapely the ankle and leg above – simply means that the lady becomes bogged down in a peat marsh. She has then to be helped out of her predicament by an unsympathetic male, who is probably shouting at his dog. It must occur to any perceptive girl that, while he is no doubt addressing his dog, he may in actual fact be referring to her. And at the top, *not* a scarlet and yellow scarf! While this may attract a non-shooting male, it repels grouse.

If appearance cannot attract as might be wished, witty conversation as an alternative should surely not be out of place. There is a snag, however: game does not like the human voice, and to talk to a man's back inevitably means raising the voice a little. And it usually is the back to which one talks, because a lady companion in the butt has to be behind the 'gun', and the 'gun' has to face to the front when game starts to come if he is to see and shoot it.

With a persistent and talkative companion, the man with the gun has either to turn round and talk to her – with his mind on the birds that he knows will come when his back is turned to them – or to face his front and hope she will soon be quiet.

Finally, her position in the butt must, she knows, be behind him. For the average female out shooting for the first time, this means the back of the butt. She is then astonished to find herself face to face with her companion as he tries to take a bird behind. This admittedly does not often happen twice, as the hot and furious eye of the 'gun' will pin her like an assegai, and she will keep out of the way in the future. But by then it may be too late.

Surely all women out on a shooting day cannot be such a nuisance? No, indeed – although some can, and are. So what advice can we give to the girl who proposes to marry the moor?

First, dress sensibly. There are clothes designed for a grouse moor, so suitable yet attractive that they can actually be noticed favourably, even if momentarily, by her companion. Unfortunately they are worn (in the writer's experience) only by married women who have served a long and hard apprenticeship.

Second, in the words of Nanny, only speak when you are spoken to. If your 'gun' is actually prepared to turn round before the drive starts, then any female will know better than I how to use the faint conversational gambit thus offered. But if the 'gun' turns away to scan his front, *shut up*!

Keep out of the way. Basically, this means being always behind him. This advice is, I fear, beyond the comprehension of many. It means being behind his back: and I will only add that to achieve this will actually involve moving around in the butt. It does not mean standing still, gazing out from the back of the butt at grouse departing rapidly to the rear: this may result in a shove of unexpected violence, with perhaps some painfully audible advice about getting out of the way.

Grouse creep up on a butt most unexpectedly. If you can warn your 'gun' of such an approach which he obviously has not seen, you will be an asset. Do it quite loudly – he may be wearing ear defenders – and keep it short. 'Half left', 'straight in front', and so on.

Can you help load? I do not mean loading with two guns, for if you can do that efficiently there is no need whatever to go on reading this, but being able to pop a couple of cartridges into a gun held open. If you propose to do this, do not wear gloves, however cold it may be. The fur of a glove jammed between barrels and the face of the breech can wreck any chance. The 'gun', hot with anxiety and excitement, will simply not understand why gloves of any description should be necessary.

If you keep well out of the way as I advise, it may be difficult to count and mark his score. To count the kills should be possible; it should even be feasible to mark them on those little score cards. If you have not got such a card, stick fired cartridges in the butt in line with where each bird has fallen.

He will forget odds and ends on leaving the butt. You will remember them, pick them up and hand them to him later — without comment.

Can you see the shot? If you can, do not delay. Marry the brute, and the moor and everybody else will benefit at once.

Final advice

Let us assume that, having finished reading this book, your reaction is that 'perhaps he has got something'. What are you going to do about it in that case? The obvious answer is, next time you are shooting, do what is written in this book, and you will become a super shot!

If it were as easy as that, most of us would be good shots. As it is, the vast majority of us are downright bad. For example, the number of men who kill consistently, *throughout the year*, more than they miss could probably be counted on the fingers of one hand. This, I admit, is not the right way to judge the skill of a shot, but at least it is an indication of the *very bad* standard of shooting prevalent.

For some reason, very few people practise shooting. In no other sport or skill do you get such a state of affairs. The golfer who slogs away, the pianist who practises for hours every day — they all do it. Yet if we see a good shot out, all we say is, 'So he ought to be; look at the practice he gets.' We are, I suppose, jealous. But, if we do not take steps to improve our shooting, we may well ask what we are shooting for.

Basically, we are too lazy. If this is true of you, you will try to kid yourself that reading this book is enough. It is quite easy to read a book – we have all practised reading enough! 'He will improve my shooting' you may say. You are making the fundamental mistake of not realising that it is your finger on the trigger, your arms and hands mounting the gun, and your body moving the gun to the bird.

In short, you cannot get away with this lazy way out. Sooner or later you have got to try and make your body comply with the wishes of your brain, which we are charitably assuming has been favourably influenced by reading this book. You have got to get down physically to putting into practice what you have read and agreed with. You must try it out, and above all practise what your brain – and only your brain – has absorbed.

The clever chap will perhaps say that this tirade is quite unnecessary. 'Such a brilliant book that even I can understand it' – painful mock modesty. Please let me repeat that this simply will not wash. The reasons are threefold.

First, you honestly believe that you are doing something I have told you, and you are *not*. The second reason is that you accept my advice with reservations; and the last is that you do not absorb, or you misunderstand, what you are being told.

Let me give an example of the last point, the non-absorption of information. This story has the merit of being quite true. I was coaching a young man, and he was shooting at the same approaching clays. I was trying to get him to *push* his gun at them; he was *lifting* his gun, and thus could not and did not keep with them as he mounted. Before every shot, I told him to push the gun at them. After twenty counted shots, I got exasperated, and held the gun near the breech when he was about to mount the gun. When the clay came over, I pushed the gun towards the clay to give him the feeling I was trying to instil. He pulled the trigger and broke the clay. He then turned to me and said, 'Oh, I see. Push the gun towards the bird. Why didn't you say so?' I wonder what he was thinking about before.

You will accept what I say with reservations. We all do it. A quick example – a shooting coach has told you that you mount your gun correctly to your cheek and shoulder. What he *meant* was that the gun was correctly mounted when it got there. He did *not* mean that you mounted correctly *with the bird*; you thought he did mean just that. So you skip the bit about gun mounting, and you get no better at shooting.

The final point: that you are not doing what you think you are. I have much experience of this, but I will give you only two examples. 'Mount the gun with the bird,' I say. After most people have fired at, say, a 'driven partridge' medium height, coming towards, I ask them whether they thought they were with it all the time they mounted. In all sincerity, they say 'Yes.' What they *did* do was to snatch the butt into the shoulder and cheek; down went the barrels, and if they had fired halfway through mounting, they would have hit the ground in front of them. I point out that the bird was never there. I am not believed. So then I hold (from behind) the whip aerial of my walkie-talkie under the gun barrels, so that if the barrels go down instead of forward and up with the bird, they will hit the aerial. When the barrels *do* hit the aerial, I am accused of flipping it up to make the 'gun' raise the barrels. None so blind as those who won't see! Are *you* blind – deliberately?

After looking at the pictures in this book of the correct and incorrect ways of standing, firing and so on, very few of us will have visualised ourselves in any of the incorrect positions. We always associate ourselves with the hero – a Walter Mitty complex. It is not whether you have ever been in one of the incorrect positions; it is *how many* of the incorrect positions you habitually adopt.

Be humble. See yourself as others see you – and become a good shot!

Glossary of Shooting Terms

Automatic   The same as a 'pump' gun (qv), except that the recocking and ejection cycle is performed automatically by recoil or gas pressure.

Box lock   A simple robust action, easily adjusted or repaired. Sometimes known as the Anson & Deeley system. Introduced in 1875. See under 'locks'.

British proof   It is illegal to sell any gun that has not been 'proofed'. Every British gun has to go to a proof house, where an abnormally heavy charge is fired from each barrel. If this test is passed, the barrel is stamped accordingly. A barrel can subsequently become 'out of proof' through wear.

Cast-off   The wooden stock of an English gun is often bent out sideways to the right, in the case of a right-handed gun, to enable the butt to fit firmly into the shoulder, and at the same time for the barrels to point where the eye is looking.

Cast-on   This is where the stock is bent to the left, for a left-handed gun, and for the same reason.

Choke   A constriction at the end of the barrel, which in the case of 'full choke' amounts to 40/1,000 of an inch. The other extreme is 'true cylinder', a term which is self-explanatory. 'Improved cylinder' has a small degree of constriction. The object is to concentrate the shot into a smaller area and thus increase the effective range; the greater the choke, the greater the reduction in the spread of the shot.

Down-the-line This is a specific clay pigeon sport. Clays are thrown at varying angles away from the 'gun', who is 16yd or more from the trap. The gun can be mounted in the shoulder and the clay is released when called for by the shooter.

Driven game The beaters drive the game towards the 'guns', who are thus offered shots at birds which may have got up a long way back, and so be flying fast and high. This type of shooting generally offers more sporting and difficult shots.

Locks The lock of a gun is responsible for causing the striker to go forward and fire the cartridge when the trigger is pulled. It also ensures that the striker is pulled back and cocked when the gun is opened, and retained in this position until the trigger is again pulled.

Mark! A warning shout that game is approaching.

Over-and-under A double-barrelled gun with its barrels placed one on top of the other. Used most often in clay pigeon shooting, for which sport it can be more easily 'aimed'. Has a tendency to be rather heavy, and the wide opening necessary to allow the lower barrel to be loaded means that not many are used for game shooting.

Pattern Guns are usually tested for pattern by firing them at a whitewashed iron plate at 40yd. The shot marks should be evenly distributed; the concentration of the pattern is determined by the percentage of the pellets in a 30in diameter circle.

'Pump' gun A single-barrelled repeating gun. The gun is recocked and the 'empty' ejected by pulling back the sliding fore-end. Usually can be loaded with five rounds, but this takes a long time. Rather clumsy to handle.

Right-and-left When a bird is shot with the right barrel, followed by a kill with the left barrel, without reloading.

Side lock Probably the best (and most expensive) form of lock. Capable of very fine adjustment, and utterly reliable and safe. A refined and thoroughbred version of the box lock. See 'locks'.

Skeet shooting A type of sporting clay pigeon shooting. There are two traps opposite each other, with the trapper suitably protected. One clay is thrown towards the other trap, when called for, and the second clay released in the opposite direction on the report of the gun. Gun positions are in a semi-circle with the first position near the higher trap. This position thus gets a going-away shot, followed immediately by a lower incomer. The halfway position gives a left-to-right crosser, followed by a right-to-left crosser. Quick shooting at comparatively short ranges is required.

Springing teal A type of clay pigeon shot in which the clay is thrown upwards at an angle of 70°. Released and shot at in the same way as down-the-line.

Stop When game is driven towards the 'guns', pheasants in particular take every opportunity of getting away by running down a ditch or hedgerow instead of flying. A man placed strategically and tapping with a stick will prevent such escapes.

Stringing The column of shot 'strings out' after leaving the barrel. At long ranges, the leading shot will be some feet ahead of the laggards.

Walking gun Where beaters are driving game towards the 'guns', it is sometimes necessary to have a 'gun' walking with the beaters to shoot birds breaking back or flying out to one side.

Walking up The 'guns' and beaters walk in line, the 'guns' shooting at birds thus disturbed. Mostly going-away shots.

Appendix I:
Pattern and Killing Power

Table 1
Minimum patterns (including allowance for stringing)

Game	Minimum pattern in a 30in circle
Snipe	270
Woodcock	150
Squirrel	180
Partridge	130
Grouse	130
Pheasant	120
Pigeon	130
Rabbit	120
Teal	110
Hare	100
Duck	80
Goose	70

Table 2
Percentage patterns for all borings at all ranges

Boring of gun	Range in yd						
	30	35	40	45	50	55	60
True cyl	60	49	40	33	27	22	18
Imp cyl	72	60	50	41	33	27	22
$\frac{1}{4}$ choke	77	65	55	46	38	30	25
$\frac{1}{2}$ choke	83	71	60	50	41	33	27
$\frac{3}{4}$ choke	91	77	65	55	46	37	30
Full choke	100	84	70	59	49	40	32

APPENDIX I

Table 3
Striking energy in ft lb for individual pellets fired at observed velocity of 1,070ft per sec

Size of shot	Range in yd						
	30	35	40	45	50	55	60
3	4·48	3·92	3·43	2·99	2·59	2·23	1·94
4	3·54	3·08	2·66	2·30	1·97	1·68	1·42
5	2·60	2·23	1·90	1·61	1·36	1·14	0·93
6	2·03	1·71	1·44	1·20	1·01	0·82	0·67
7	1·52	1·27	1·06	0·86	0·70	0·57	0·45

Table 4
Diameter of spread (being the diameter in inches covered by the bulk of the charge of a gun at various ranges for all calibres*)

Boring of gun	Range in yd						
	10	15	20	25	30	35	40
True cyl	20	26	32	38	44	51	58
Imp cyl	15	20	26	32	38	44	51
$\frac{1}{4}$ choke	13	18	23	29	35	41	48
$\frac{1}{2}$ choke	12	16	21	26	32	38	45
$\frac{3}{4}$ choke	10	14	18	23	29	35	42
Full choke	9	12	16	21	27	33	40

*Note: Because of the persistent fallacy that small-bore guns throw a smaller pattern circle than those of larger bore, it is necessary to emphasise that this is not the case. All bores throw approximately the same diameter circle, and the above table is therefore true for all calibres, as stated.

Appendix II:
Suggested Rules for a Clay Pigeon Club

1   The title of the club shall be the '............ Clay Pigeon Club'.
2   The headquarters of the club shall be at ....
3   The object and aim of the club shall be to improve the standard of game shooting among members.
4   The management of the club shall be vested in a chairman and in a committee of five, three of whom shall form a quorum, who shall be elected from the members of the club at each annual general meeting. Retiring members shall be eligible for re-election.
5   A president and vice-president shall be elected from the members of the club at each annual general meeting, and the retiring president and vice-president shall be eligible for re-election.
6   The committee shall have the power to add to the number of vice-presidents for the current year.
7   An honorary treasurer and honorary secretary shall be elected from the members at each annual general meeting, and the retiring honorary treasurer and honorary secretary shall be eligible for re-election.
8   The committee shall have power to fill any vacancies on the committee during the current year, and also have power to form sub-committees as may be required for special purposes.
9   The president and vice-president shall be *ex officio* members of the committee, but the vice-president shall not have voting powers. The honorary treasurer and honorary secretary shall be *ex officio* members of all committees with full voting powers.
10   All monies received on behalf of the club shall forthwith be paid into the account of the club at the .... Bank. The honorary treasurer shall have power to draw on such account, and no cheque shall be drawn by him unless countersigned by another official and previously sanctioned by resolution of the committee. No prizes or other articles shall be purchased, or debts or liabilities incurred on behalf of the club by any person, without

the previous sanction of a resolution of the committee or at a general meeting of the club.

11   The accounts of the club shall be audited every year by auditors to be appointed at a general meeting of the club. A copy of the accounts so audited shall be sent to every member of the club at least seven days before the annual general meeting of the club.

12   The subscription of the club shall be £4 per annum, with an entrance fee of £4 for the first year. The financial year of the club shall be from 1 April until 31 March the following year.

13   The annual general meeting of the club shall be held on or after the last week in March each year, and fourteen days' notice shall be given to all members. Resolutions to be proposed at the meeting shall be given in writing to the honorary secretary seven clear days before the date of the meeting.

14   On a petition signed by at least one-third of the members of the club being presented in writing to the honorary secretary, a special general meeting shall be called within fourteen days from the date of presentation of the petition to consider the matter contained therein.

15   The committee shall have power to form such bye-laws as they consider will be conducive to the good of the club, and to the encouragement of this sport.

16   A candidate for election shall be proposed and seconded by members of the club, who shall submit his name and address to the committee. The committee shall vote thereon at the first committee meeting subsequent to the one at which his application for membership was submitted, unless the committee unanimously resolve the vote thereon at the committee meeting at which such application was received by them.

17   Any member whose subscription is unpaid from 1 May shall not be allowed any of the privileges of membership. The committee may strike out names of members whose subscriptions are more than two months in arrears.

18   Members shall, subject to the consent of all members present, have the right of introducing visitors to club practice, provided that any member introducing a visitor shall be liable for all debts incurred by him to the club. No visitors shall be invited to practise or shoot more than three times in the same season. No member may introduce more than two visitors at the same time.

19   The committee shall be empowered to request the resignation of a member if it be proved to their satisfaction that his conduct merits it; and, in the event of his failing to resign, the committee

may suspend such member without further notice. The resolution calling on a member to be suspended should be carried by the votes of the majority of the members present and voting, notwithstanding anything herein contained to the contrary as regards a quorum or otherwise. Such a suspension may only be reviewed at a general meeting.

20 Members must use such targets as may be decided upon by the club.

21 A range officer approved by the committee must be appointed for each club shoot.

22 It is a condition of membership that the club will not be held responsible (except as covered by insurance) for any accident and/or injury occurring to or caused by either members or visitors.

23 The committee are empowered to make or alter any rule which may be found necessary to conform with the Licensing (Consolidation) Act 1910, and such rule shall forthwith become a rule of the club as if it has been passed at a general meeting.

24 These rules shall be open to revision during the first year of the club by the committee, but after that no alteration shall be made except by resolution at the annual general meeting.

25 Temporary members may be elected for a period of one month. They must be proposed and seconded by a member and elected by the committee. The fee for such membership shall be 50p.

26 In the event of the club being disbanded, all the assets of the club shall be liquidated and equally divided among the full members on the books of the club at that date.

Index

INDEX

INDEX